cooking
on the farm

Katie Khoury

cooking
on the farm

katie khoury

Recipes from the Rooster Ranch Hunt Club

copyright 2013 by Katie Khoury

Katie Khoury
for more information and recipes please visit:
littlespatula.blogspot.com

to visit the Rooster Ranch Hunt Club contact:
R. Kim Anthony
Rooster Ranch Hunt Club
7480 Germania Road
Ubly, Michigan 48475
(989) 658-2332
http://www.huntrr.com

for my mom & dad

contents

Introduction

The Rooster Ranch Hunt Club is located in Ubly, a rural farming community in the Thumb of Michigan. My father, Kim Anthony and our family developed the hunting preserve from the ground up in the mid 1980's. In 1986 my father sat at the kitchen table with my mother, my younger brother Nick (5), myself (7) and my older brother Matt (9) and shared with us an idea that he had been thinking about for quite some time.

We had grown up listening to my dad tell stories about his childhood so when he began reminiscing about pheasant hunting long ago as a child, we sat at the kitchen table listening intently, but at the same time very curious as to where he was leading us. What big idea was he about to share with us? He said he missed the land he knew as a child that was chuck full of game birds, small game, and trophy deer. He explained that we could recreate the land he remembered by growing game birds and filling the land with them. We could invite hunters to come experience pheasant hunting the way it once was and welcome them to land with lush fields laden with cackling pheasants.

He was so excited by this new prospect that we also began to believe that this could become a reality. We could make a living from our own farmland, and we could all stake a claim in the new venture's birth if we pitched in. It sounded like there was going to be plenty of work to go around.

The first piece of business that we attended to was naming this new business of ours. My dad encouraged each of us to come up with a few possible names. We each wrote down potential names on slips of paper and threw them in a hat. He pulled each one out and read them aloud. Out of the many suggestions, many silly plays on words, we came away with The Rooster Ranch. And that is how we began everything. If only the rest was so easy!

That year we grew our first batch of pheasants in a small barn located close to our home so that the baby chicks could be monitored throughout those first unstable nights. We prepped the barns with straw, rings, heat lamps, waterers, and feeders. The 500 baby chicks were brought to us by truck, and we carefully unloaded the boxes of peeping chicks. We marveled at their softness, we held them, and we petted them. We were delighted by the huge number of chicks we were about to raise. We knew little about raising fowl, but we learned quickly and had success that first year and the years following. We experimented with incubating our own eggs for a short while with mixed results. We dabbled in raising everything from quail to turkeys and ducks, but pheasants were our main priority. Now, over two decades later, the ranch gets delivery upwards of 30,000 day old chicks trucked in from Ohio every spring and through the summer months.

After experimenting those first few years, my father's main objective was to grow the business and create a positive hunting experience for every single person to step foot on our ranch. In order to achieve that goal he put us to work renovating barns, building flight pens, adding dog runs, and planting cover. We spent each summer completing projects to better the land and the ranch.

Over time we slowly renovated the barn we used those early years to raise our 500 chicks into a clubhouse for hunters to gather and meet before and after a day of hunting. The first few years my brothers would guide hunts, and I would help them clean pheasants on a small counter behind the barn. As business picked up and the number of pheasants we grew increased, my dad and brothers were able to add a heated cleaning room to the clubhouse. My brothers and I picked stones one summer to help create a large stone fireplace in the back room of the clubhouse. We also added a large kitchen with a walk in cooler years later that my mother now uses to serve breakfast, lunch, and dinner to hunters as well as staff and family, adding up to over a thousand meals each year.

We all worked tirelessly as kids, and we each found our niche. My older brother Matt has become the king of construction. Over time he has taught himself how to construct nearly every structure on the ranch. As kids we would sit at the table and look at sketches he had come up with for a new flight pen, dog run, or a kitchen renovation. He has always loved a good challenge and has always been able to transform Dad's rough ideas into actual structures. Even off the ranch he has been able to renovate his entire home as well as lodges and an office space for his wife's photography business in town. He is also more than capable with a big piece of equipment. He has made moving dirt into a profession. He plows snow in the winter to keep the ranch accessible and clears land in the summer to create ponds, watering holes, and new features on the ranch.

My younger brother has always had a knack for the actual sport of hunting. He is a terrific shot with a gun, and he's still pretty good with a bow and arrow. As a kid he would outshoot all of the older guys at the gun club, and he would proudly bring home patches to prove his prowess. He has quite a collection of perfect score patches. He has always been a real guys' guy and enjoys guiding hunts, training dogs, and working the business end of things. He still gets in there and works, but I know he enjoys getting other people to do the dirty work for him whenever possible.

As for me, I have always loved being involved in the technical end of things at the ranch. I spent many hours as a kid entering client information into spreadsheets to create mailing lists and flyers. When I wasn't busy with that I was expected to help out in the kitchen cooking alongside my mother. We would make big batches of chili, copious amounts of macaroni salad, and a sea of sheet cakes to serve during tower hunts every weekend. I happened to enjoy that time very much and developed a love for cooking that grew stronger as I grew older and became more independent in the kitchen. Over time, I honed my skills and cooking became part of my identity. So it is very fitting that I create this cookbook filled with recipes that I grew up eating as well as some new recipes that I have created for my own family.

As much as my father, brothers, and I worked on the ranch, the real lifeblood has always been my mother. She is essential to the ranch in so many ways, and it would be impossible to run it without her. She not only cooks the meals that feed the family, but she also prepares food to nourish hunters on the ranch. She works tirelessly through the night tending to the chicks those first few weeks and on through all of their life stages. She also has the huge task of maintaining the clubhouse, grounds, and livestock through all four seasons. I have watched her my entire life, and I believe that she is the hardest working woman I will ever know.

Black Flies

When I was a kid we had an old yellow boat that we would hitch to our Bronco and drive up to the lake every summer. My father was always eager to get to the lake early in the morning before the sun came up. He wanted to get the boat on the water while the fish were biting and head home before the heat set in at midday. Being a notorious night-owl, I loathed waking up that early. I especially disliked the gruff manner with which he would wake me up. With no warning, my dad would flip on the light next to my bed and yell out "Get up, we're leaving." I'm guessing my brothers down the hall got the same wake up call, and we were given about 1 minute to get in the car before he started driving away. With a shared bathroom between the 3 of us, it was tricky to make it outside before Dad started driving away.

When we finally came running out of the house, we would have to chase after the car. Dad would stop the car just briefly enough for us to get our hands on the back door, and just as we were about to open it he would let up on the break so that the car would lurch forward, and we would lose our grip on the handle. Then he would stop and repeat the whole thing 5 or 6 times until he had all of us exasperated and shaking our heads in frustration. I know that my dad enjoyed tormenting us and was most likely laughing to himself in the car. I put up with it because I had no choice; he was my dad and I did love the lake so I went along with the whole charade.

My favorite part about being on the boat were the times that my dad would let me steer the boat while we were trolling for fish. I used to get the biggest kick out of talking to people over the cb radio. My brothers and I used to sing our own rendition of a Buck Owens song we had heard on Hee Haw. Our version only consisted of the chorus;

Where, oh where, are you tonight?
Why did you leave me here all alone?
I searched the world over and thought I'd found true love.
You met another and PTHHP! you was gone.

and we would sing it over and over into the radio. I don't even know if anyone could hear us, but we found it ridiculously funny and we would laugh until our sides hurt. Oddly, that song was a highlight of my childhood and my brothers and I still sing it when we're together.

One particularly cold morning dad herded us into the car and drove us up to the lake excited to try out his new planer boards. My mom, brothers, and I wrapped ourselves in blankets and huddled in the cabin while Dad drove the boat miles and miles out into the middle of the lake. My older brother suffered from motion sickness, and he would always turn a shade of green during the drive out. I also found it hard to keep from feeling sick and tried to focus on anything but the rhythmic thud of the boat hitting the waves and the sharp turns Dad would make from time to time.

After what seemed like hours of powering over and through sizable waves, we finally stopped and Dad began setting up the fishing rods and new planer boards. He let the planer boards out with plenty of line; and we waited inside the cabin as he fiddled with his new setup. After quite awhile he called out to Mom and I to come hold the planer boards. He had forgotten the proper equipment he needed to set up his new boards, and he had no way of securing them to the sides of the boat. He was so determined to try out his new boards that he told us to sit still and hold the lines steady and keep the planer boards in position.

What he failed to tell us was that the lake was swarming with black flies that morning. As soon as my mother and I opened the hatch we were surrounded by millions of tiny black flies. They were everywhere. The air around us was so thick with flies that we could not open our mouths for fear of swallowing a mouthful of tiny black flies. We tried to protest, but Dad was insistent that we hold the lines. We zipped up our sweatshirts and pulled our hoods over our heads and climbed onto the bow of the boat. The black flies swarmed around us. We could feel them crawling on our faces, up our noses, in our eyes, and we could hear them buzzing in our ears. We swatted at them and tried to move our arms and legs continuously to keep them from landing on us, but nothing worked. We pulled our hoods even tighter and tied the strings so

14

that only our noses poked through. No matter how hard we tried, the flies still managed to get inside our hoods. They were everywhere but Dad insisted that we keep holding the line.

To make matters worse, Dad started catching fish, which meant that we were not going to head back to shore anytime soon. So Mom and I sat in complete agony for hours while my dad and brothers reeled in fish. I honestly do not know how they managed to stay out there for so long because Mom and I could not take it. After hours of begging him to take us to shore, I think I was in tears at one point, he finally said he would. We just needed to reel in all of the lines. Mom and I were so relieved! We pulled in the planer boards and did a happy dance.

We each took a pole and started reeling furiously. At first my line was slack and I was reeling as fast as I possibly could. Then I felt it catch suddenly. The line started to make a zipping sound as it was pulled away from the boat. Immediately I could tell that I had hooked a big fish. I got myself set and called out to everyone, so that they could watch the fight and get the net ready. I knew that it was going to be a big walleye by how hard it pulled on my line. I fought as it pulled away from me, taking a bit more line. Slowly and steadily, I reeled the fish in making sure not to let the line go slack. I tried to remember everything Dad had taught me, all the while praying that I didn't lose the fish. I don't think there is anything more disappointing than losing a huge fish during a good fight. I could feel how big my walleye was, and I was excited to see it finally surface.

After a terrific battle the fish finally surfaced. Dad scooped up my walleye with his net and brought it into the boat. Thankful and relieved that I didn't lose the battle, I could finally breathe a sigh of relief. We all marveled at my catch, and for a few seconds I completely forgot about those pesky flies and I had a marvelous time. I remember the look of joy on my dad's face in that moment, and it almost made the whole torturous day worth it. But, after the initial excitement subsided, I felt those black flies swarm around me again. I told Dad to take me and my monster fish to shore as soon as possible.

Chapter 1 ✳ Breakfast

I love breakfast. I love that there are so many options to choose from and many are quick fixes. Whether you like something sweet, salty, spicy, or creamy anything goes for your first meal of the day. One of my favorite breakfast dishes is a spin on Eggs Benedict with a crisp English muffin, warm salty ham, and creamy poached egg all topped with a slightly spicy homemade queso.

I can't say that I haven't eaten a plate of apple Danish, raspberry pie, or strawberry shortcake in the morning. My mother is especially guilty of having dessert for breakfast. More than once I've seen her take a bite of pie and then turn to me claiming that it contains plenty of fruit so it is perfectly acceptable for breakfast. I guess I can't argue with that.

Barb's Granola

My mom has been making a version of this granola for years and years. Everyone loves it and people ask her for the recipe every time she makes it. I started making it on my own not too long after I tasted hers. I often double the recipe and freeze a portion of it since I like to have it around for a quick breakfast. I just take a jar out and let it defrost on the counter for an hour or two, and then I store it in the pantry for easy access. I've found that if I get low I tend to hoard it and leave it in the freezer where no one will see it so I can sneak a handful of frozen granola to top my morning yogurt.

4 cups rolled oats
½ cup brown sugar
2 teaspoons cinnamon
½ cup honey
1 ½ cups chopped nuts*
1 ½ cups dried fruit
½ teaspoon salt
¼ cup olive oil
1 teaspoon vanilla

Preheat oven to 250°F. Mix oats, sugar, cinnamon, salt, and chopped nuts in a large bowl. Combine honey and oil in a heatproof measuring cup and microwave for 30 seconds, whisk in the vanilla. Drizzle oil mixture over the oat and nut mixture and toss to coat. Bake on a parchment lined baking sheet for 50 minutes. Use a rubber spatula to stir the mixture every 10 minutes. Remove from oven and let cool completely. Carefully break up granola and mix in dried fruits. Store in a mason jar at room temperature or freeze for up to 3 months.

*I like a mix of chopped walnuts, pecans, and slivered almonds.

Muesli

The granola recipe on the preceding page is absolutely perfect on top of this muesli. Now, if you haven't ever had muesli don't knock it. I wasn't too sure about it either, and it took a couple of tries before I started to really enjoy it, but now I absolutely love it. Cold soaked oats just sound bad, but it is quite tasty once it is topped with yogurt, fruit, and a handful of granola. Try it at least twice before you make up your mind about it.

¼ cup rolled oats
¼ cup apple juice
¼ cup yogurt
fruit
granola

Spoon the rolled oats and apple juice into a small jar with a lid. Gently stir or shake a bit to combine. Top with yogurt and berries. Store in the refrigerator overnight or up to 3 days. Top with granola just before eating.

*I have found that I can prepare 3 to 4 on Sunday night and eat them during the week. They are perfectly portioned and portable so eating them on the go is quite easy.

*A bit of jam makes a good substitute for fruit if you do not have any on hand.

Chocolate Chip Scones

These are a family favorite that the kids go bonkers over every time I make them. They love the fact that they get to eat chocolate for breakfast. I've also made them with dried cranberries; and they are pretty spectacular, and my mother actually prefers them over the chocolate chip variety.

They can easily be prepped the night before and baked the next day if you don't have time to mess with mixing bowls and pastry cutters first thing in the morning. Just be sure to add the coarse sugar just before baking.

These scones can also be made without any chocolate chips or fruit and then used as a biscuit base for strawberry shortcake.

2 cups all purpose flour
¼ cup sugar
2 teaspoons baking powder
¼ teaspoon baking soda
5 ½ tablespoons cold butter
½ teaspoon salt
1 egg
½ cup buttermilk*
⅓ cup chocolate chips
2 teaspoons decorating sugar
1 tablespoon buttermilk

Preheat oven to 400°F. Whisk dry ingredients together in a large bowl. Cut cold butter into dry mixture with a pastry cutter or fork. Mix buttermilk and egg in a small bowl, add to flour mixture. Mix briefly with a fork, then add chocolate chips. Using your fork, gently mix until flour mixture begins to come together and forms a shaggy ball. Use your hands to gently incorporate remaining flour, add a tablespoon more buttermilk if necessary. Be sure to handle the dough as gently and as briefly as possible. The more you handle it the tougher the final product will be.

Line a round pizza pan with parchment paper and pat dough into a disc about 1 inch thick. Use a large knife to cut into 6 pieces in the same manner you would cut a pizza. Separate each scone so they are about one inch apart. Brush wedges with a bit of buttermilk and sprinkle with coarse sugar. Bake for 12 minutes or until edges are browned.

*If you don't have buttermilk you can make your own by measuring out regular milk and adding a tablespoon of vinegar to it. Let it sit for about 5-10 minutes so that it can curdle before using.

*You can also substitute whole cream for the buttermilk.

Banana Bread Muffins

These muffins are so tasty and make a terrific breakfast. The extras also freeze beautifully. Place any surplus in a ziplock bag and store in the freezer. Defrost at room temperature for an hour or heat in a 350°F oven for 5-6 minutes, if desired.

I like to bake mine in mini loaf pans. Each loaf is about the size of a large cupcake, and everyone can have their own. If you don't have or can't find mini loaf pans, you can easily bake them in cupcakes pans.

3 cups all purpose flour
1 teaspoon baking soda
1 teaspoon salt
½ teaspoon baking powder
½ teaspoon cinnamon
½ teaspoon fresh nutmeg
1 ½ cups sugar
1 cup vegetable oil
3 eggs
1 tablespoon vanilla
4 ripe bananas, peeled and mashed
½ cup walnuts, chopped (optional)
1 cup chocolate chips (optional)

Preheat oven to 325°F. Whisk the dry ingredients in a medium bowl. Beat the oil, sugar, eggs, and vanilla in a stand mixer until blended. Add the dry ingredients and blend until just incorporated. Mix in the banana.

Spray the mini loaf pans with baking spray and equally divide batter between them. Bake for 25 minutes or until a toothpick inserted into the center comes out clean.

*Muffin pans will also work and will bake for about 20-25 minutes.

*Mini muffins work well too and bake for 15-18 minutes.

Cinnamon Swirl Bread
makes 2 loaves

6 ⅔ cups all purpose flour
½ cup wheat germ
4 teaspoons salt
4 teaspoons active dry yeast
4 tablespoons olive oil
2 tablespoons honey
2 ⅓ cups very warm water
6 tablespoons butter, softened
1 tablespoon cinnamon
1 cup sugar

In a measuring cup add olive oil and honey, then fill with enough warm water to measure 2½ cups. In the bowl of a stand mixer, with a dough hook, add the flour, wheat germ, salt, and the yeast. Mix with a spatula. Turn mixer on low and slowly add the wet ingredients.

Increase speed to medium and mix for a few minutes until dough comes together and pulls away from the sides of the bowl. (If dough is dry add a tablespoon of water at a time until it just comes together.)

Lower speed a notch and knead for 6-8 minutes. Remove dough and form into a ball. Place in a large greased bowl and cover for 1½ to 2 hours or until doubled in size. (Place dough in a warm area.)

Divide dough into two portions. Turn one portion of dough onto counter (I line mine with plastic wrap for easy clean-up) and flatten into a large rectangle about ½ inch thick. Spread a bit of butter on the dough and then sprinkle generously with sugar and cinnamon. Roll short end to short end, tuck ends under and place in a buttered loaf pan seam-side down. Repeat with remaining dough.

Cover dough and place in a warm area to rise for 1 hour. Preheat oven to 350° and bake breads for about 35 minutes. Remove and let cool 15 minutes before slicing.

Eggs with Sweet Corn, Spinach, and Hollandaise

I came up with this breakfast one summer when I had a surplus of fresh corn in the fridge. I love how the creamy egg yolk and hollandaise coat the fresh sweet corn. It is a knockout combination. Having said that, you must make this dish with fresh sweet corn from the garden, farmer's market, or a roadside stand as frozen or canned corn does not burst in your mouth like fresh corn.

1 ½ cups fresh corn kernels, cut off cob
2 cups baby spinach leaves
4 eggs
1 tablespoon butter
kosher salt
freshly ground black pepper
hollandaise sauce, prepared (see page 30)

In a small sauté pan add a pat of butter and melt. Add corn and spinach and cook until spinach is wilted and corn is heated through. Season with salt and pepper and then transfer to serving plates.

Wipe pan with paper towel if desired and add a second small pat of butter and fry the eggs. Place cooked eggs on top of corn mixture and top with hollandaise sauce. Serve with toasted pita bread.

Hollandaise Sauce

5 tablespoons butter
1 egg yolk
½ to 1 tablespoon fresh lemon juice
kosher salt
hot sauce

Heat butter in microwave safe bowl until just barely melted. Lumps should be visible and you should stir to finish melting. Do not let it get too hot or it will separate. In a blender, combine egg yolk, ½ tablespoon lemon juice, a pinch of salt, and a dash of hot sauce. Blend until the sauce is a pale yellow. Open the pour spout in the blender and drizzle in the melted butter a few drops at a time and blend until incorporated. Continue adding butter in small quantities until all of the butter is added. Taste and add more lemon juice if desired. You may thin the sauce with a few drops of water.

*Feel free to double this recipe.

Crepes

makes 12-14 small crepes

Crepes can be fun to make. Just go into it knowing that the first one almost always ends up in the garbage. Once you have the temperature right then you can make them up quite quickly and keep them in a warm oven covered with a dish towel until you're ready to serve. I like to make savory ones with ham and cheese as well as sweet ones with chocolate and strawberries.

1 ½ cups milk
2 eggs
1 cup flour
½ teaspoon kosher salt
½ teaspoon baking powder
1 tablespoon sugar

Whisk eggs, milk, and sugar together in a medium bowl. Add dry ingredients and whisk vigorously until combined. Heat a small 8" pan over medium heat and spray with cooking spray. Pour a scant ¼ cup batter and immediately lift and tilt pan and swirl the batter around and around to coat the pan. The batter should be quite thin. Cook for about 2 minutes or until edges are dry and beginning to brown. Flip with a spatula and cook for 20 seconds on the second side. Remove, place on an oven-safe pan, cover with a clean towel and keep in a 200°F oven. Repeat with remaining batter.

*Fill with bananas and chocolate chips for a sweet breakfast or dessert crepe and ham and cheese for a savory breakfast crepe.

Eggs Benedict con Queso

serves 2

The first time I served this I was trying to make a quick breakfast for company that was in a rush to leave before a big snowfall. I didn't have time to make hollandaise so I topped it with cheese sauce leftover from the night before. Now we prefer our Eggs Benedict this way.

2 tablespoons butter
2 tablespoons flour
½ onion, diced
1 clove garlic, minced
½ jalapeño pepper, diced
8 ounces white American cheese
½ cup heavy cream
kosher salt
freshly ground black pepper
2 eggs
2 slices ham
2 English muffins
cilantro, optional

In a small saucepan melt butter. Add onion and jalapeño and sauté until tender. Add garlic and flour and sauté 2 minutes more. Whisk in cream and slowly add grated cheese a little at a time. Season with salt and pepper, if necessary. If cheese sauce is too thick add a bit more cream.

Toast English muffin, heat ham, and poach the eggs. Layer them in that order and top with cheese sauce and fresh cilantro, if desired.

*White American cheese can be found at the deli counter.

How to Poach an Egg

I learned this little trick one day while watching an old rerun of Julia Childs. She dropped an egg, with the shell still on, in boiling water for about 3 seconds. Then she removed it and cracked the egg and dropped it in the water to poach. I found that leaving the eggs in the water 10 seconds worked even better.

I don't think I'm smarter than Julia, I just think she was using room temperature eggs. I never plan ahead enough to have my eggs at room temperature when cooking breakfast, and I'm guessing most of you don't either.

1 small saucepan
1-4 fresh eggs
1 tablespoon vinegar

Bring a small pot of water to a gentle boil. Add one tablespoon of white vinegar. Gently drop each egg (up to four eggs at one time) into the water. Slowly count to ten and then remove eggs with a slotted spoon. Crack each egg into a small dish. Gently tip the egg into the simmering water. Repeat with additional eggs. Poach for 3 minutes and then remove with a slotted spoon.

*I have done these in advance and then simply slipped them back into the hot water for a few seconds so that I can serve everyone at the same time.

*Toasted pita bread spread with ripe avocado and topped with a poached egg is another delicious breakfast.

Biscuits (and Gravy)

makes about 6 biscuits

My mom makes really terrific biscuits and gravy. The gravy is full of flavorful sausage and it is delicious and filling. She and my brothers work outside tending to the farm most days so they get to indulge often since they're working off all of those calories. I, however, have to save these as a special treat and only make them occasionally.

Serve these tender biscuits with sausage gravy, or do what I do and slather on some homemade jam and you'll be in heaven!

Buttermilk Biscuits

2 cups self rising flour*
⅓ cup shortening
⅔ cup buttermilk
½ teaspoon kosher salt
2 tablespoons melted butter

Heat oven to 450°F. Sift flour and salt into a large bowl and then cut shortening into flour with a pastry cutter or a fork. Add buttermilk and stir with a fork until it forms a shaggy ball. Use your hands to gather dough and knead two to three times until flour is incorporated. Roll out and cut biscuits with a drinking glass. Place on a parchment lined pan. Bake for 10-12 minutes or until light golden brown. Remove from oven and brush with melted butter.

*Make you own self rising flour by sifting 1 cup cake flour, 1 cup all purpose flour, 1 teaspoon salt, and 3 teaspoons baking powder.

Sausage Gravy

Feel free to substitute other wild game sausage for the pork sausage. Wild boar or wild turkey sausage mixed with pork sausage would be a good place to start.

1 ½ pounds pork
2 tablespoons butter
½ cup flour
4 cups milk
freshly ground black pepper
2 teaspoons fresh thyme

Melt butter in a skillet. Add sausage and cook until browned. Be sure to break it up into small pieces with the side of a wooden spoon as it cooks. Stir in flour and cook for 3-4 minutes more. Slowly whisk in the milk and simmer until thickened. Season with thyme and freshly ground pepper.

Buttermilk Pancakes

Buttermilk makes these pancakes fluffy and tender. Top them with chocolate chips, honey, or raspberry sauce for a decadent weekend breakfast. My personal favorite combination is sliced bananas, walnuts, and honey.

2 cups flour
2 tablespoons sugar
2 teaspoons baking powder
1 teaspoon baking soda
1 teaspoon kosher salt
2 eggs
2 cups buttermilk
3 tablespoons butter, melted
1 teaspoon vanilla

Whisk dry ingredients in a large bowl. In a separate bowl whisk together the wet ingredients. Slowly add wet ingredients to dry and beat until incorporated. Lumps may remain. Preheat griddle or large pan and oil lightly. Add ⅓ cup batter and spread into a circle. When the top is very bubbly and edges are dry, flip pancake over and cook 1 minute more. Repeat with remaining batter.

Oven Fries with Green Onions

These oven fries make a great side dish for omelets or scrambled eggs. Use this recipe as a guide and experiment with different spices to make it your own.

3-4 large potatoes
1 tablespoon flour
¼ cup Parmesan cheese
1 teaspoon kosher salt
½ freshly ground black pepper
1 teaspoon smoked paprika
2-3 tablespoons olive oil
1-2 green onions, sliced thinly (reserved)

Heat oven to 400°F.   Wash potatoes and cut into wedges.   Drop onto a sheet pan lined with parchment paper. Add all remaining ingredients and toss with hands.   Spread out into a single layer and bake 25-35 minutes (depending on thickness of potatoes) until potatoes are cooked through and browned on edges. Pull out of oven and add green onion.

Vegetable Hash Topped with a Poached Egg

I ordered this for breakfast at a diner a few years ago and I immediately went home and made my own version of it. Once you cut into the poached egg the yolk spills out over the vegetables and covers them with a creamy lusciousness that makes everything come together and taste absolutely delicious. It is also packed full of healthy vegetables that make you feel good about starting your day.

1 sweet potato, peeled and diced
4-6 small Yukon gold potatoes, washed and quartered
1 red bell pepper, large dice
1 small onion, large dice
1 cup cauliflower, cut into bite sized pieces
½ pound Brussels sprouts, halved or quartered
4 eggs, poached
fresh rosemary or thyme, minced
1-2 tablespoons butter
olive oil
kosher salt
freshly ground black pepper

Preheat oven to 400°F. Toss vegetables with a tablespoon of olive oil. Season with salt, pepper, and rosemary. Roast in hot oven for 15-20 minutes or until vegetables are tender. Transfer hot vegetables to a large bowl and add butter. Mix and taste for seasonings. Portion vegetable mixture onto four plates and top each with a poached egg.

*Alternately, roast in a cast iron pan and then serve hash in the pan with poached eggs arranged on top.

*Vegetables may be steamed instead of roasted for a lighter option.

*Top with hollandaise for a less healthy, but delicious option.

The Crusher Claw

We've always had a large, rotating staff at the ranch. We hire seasonal help much of the time, and a lot of our staff happens to be friends or family. Some people trade their services for the chance to pheasant hunt, others enjoy guiding hunts or like working part time. At any given moment we have at least a dozen people that do a variety of jobs on the ranch. There are people needed to guide hunts, run the cleaning room, help serve meals, maintain the grounds, help with chores, clean lodges, and a vast array of other projects that come and go throughout the year.

Every year my dad hosts a staff holiday party in the clubhouse and invites everyone that has worked on the ranch during the season to bring their families for dinner. We usually serve a nice meal of steaks or a big prime rib with all the sides. One year dad decided to go big and ordered live Maine lobster that he had flown in fresh.

On the day of the party, a delivery truck came by and dropped off 3 or 4 styrofoam travel coolers packed with the live lobsters. Dad had ordered two dozen lobsters and my brothers and I snuck into where they were stored to check on them. We opened up one cooler and carefully took a look at them. They seemed quite lethargic and had their claws restricted with rubber bands so we thought nothing of picking up a couple to play with them. We touched their bellies and watched them flip their tails and move their antenna. Delighted and satisfied, we put them back in the cooler and left.

Later that evening, when all of the staff and their families had arrived, my dad brought the coolers into the clubhouse. Oblivious to the fact that we had already checked them out, he grabbed one of the lobsters and started to inspect it just like we had done earlier. Then he warned my brothers and I to be careful with them because they were powerful even though they looked lethargic. We gave each other sly glances as he went on about the lobsters. He explained that they have two types of claws, each with a different purpose. The smaller pincher claw is what they use to grasp food and the larger crusher claw is used to open hard-shelled foods like clams and sea urchins. He mentioned that their crusher claws were massively strong and that they could easily break a pencil or even a finger in half.

Within seconds of his warning, one of the hunting guides emerged from the back room and saw my dad holding up a lobster. Excited and intrigued by the creature, he came over and grabbed one. Before dad had a chance to stop him, he took the blue rubber band off the lobster's crusher claw. Figuring it was too lethargic to do any damage, he put his finger out for the lobster to grab. Just like dad had said, the lobster came to life and grabbed the guide's finger and proceeded to crush it. The guide screamed and dropped to his knees in pain, and my dad frantically sent my brothers to get pliers. They quickly used the pliers to grab onto the lobster's claw and pry it open, releasing the guide's finger. The guide was shaken, and luckily his pride was the only thing that was hurt. As you can imagine, he got quite a bit of grief from everyone at the party that night.

I do not believe that my dad has ever served live lobster at a Christmas party since that day. I, however, send my dad two live lobsters every year on his birthday and we always have a good chuckle about the year he served live lobster at the staff Christmas party.

Chapter 2 ✳ Soups

There is just something about a steaming bowl of soup on a cold day that comforts a person. Soup also happens to be one of my favorite things to cook because I almost always have the ingredients on hand. I like that each one starts with basic ingredients but turns into a hearty and comforting meal.

Soup is served at the ranch throughout the winter months. Hunters can stop in any time of day and warm up in the clubhouse with a warm bowl of soup and a handful of crackers.

Minestrone

Sometimes I add a chunk of Parmesan cheese rind with the broth and allow it to simmer with the vegetables. I remove it at the same time as the bay leaf, and I find that it gives the soup an added layer of flavor.

2 tablespoons olive oil
1 tablespoon bacon fat (optional)
1 large onion, diced
2 cups carrots, peeled and sliced
1 ½ cups celery, sliced
3 cloves garlic, minced
4 sprigs fresh thyme
1 (26 ounce) can whole peeled tomatoes
1 large zucchini, cubed
8 cups chicken stock
1 bay leaf
kosher salt
freshly ground black pepper
1 (15 ounce) can cannellini beans
2 cups small pasta, cooked
grated Parmesan cheese

Heat olive oil (and bacon fat, if using) in a large pot or Dutch oven and add the onions, carrots, celery, garlic, and thyme. Cook over medium heat for 8-10 minutes or until vegetables begin to soften. Using your hands, crush the tomatoes as you add them to the pot.

Add the chicken stock, bay leaf, a tablespoon of salt, a teaspoon of pepper and simmer for 30-40 minutes. Remove the bay leaf and add the beans and zucchini. Simmer an additional 10 minutes or until zucchini is cooked to your liking. Taste and season again, if desired, remove bay leaf and discard. Add a large spoonful of pasta to the bottom of each bowl and ladle soup over as you serve it. Serve with a sprinkle of Parmesan cheese.

Fish Chowder

Jane, my mom's cousin, has always been like an aunt to my brothers and me. She has been there for all of the big events in our lives and has spent many holidays with us. She is also always willing to lend a hand whenever extra help is needed at the ranch, and I always look forward to her spunky personality when I visit. This is my take on her fish chowder.

2 slices bacon, chopped
4 tablespoons butter
1 (8 ounce) salmon filet, skin removed and cut into 1 inch pieces
1 cup chopped onion
1 ½ cups potatoes, peeled and diced
½ cup chopped celery
1 cup carrots, peeled and sliced
12 ounces fresh mushrooms, sliced
1 teaspoon salt
½ teaspoon pepper
2 cups heavy cream, warmed
1 cup evaporated milk

Cook bacon in a heavy bottomed Dutch oven or soup pot. Once the fat is rendered, remove the crisp bacon and drain on a paper towel-lined plate.

Add onion, celery, salt, and pepper and cook 4-5 minutes, or until translucent. Add potatoes, carrots, mushrooms, bay leaf, and thyme and just enough water (about 2 ½ cups) to cover vegetables. Bring up to a boil and then turn heat down. Simmer for 10-15 minutes, or until vegetables are tender.

Season fish with salt and pepper, add to soup along with the warmed cream and milk. Heat, but do not boil, until salmon is cooked through, about 10 minutes. Gently break up salmon pieces with a wooden spoon, remove bay leaf, and garnish with bacon.

*The cream can be microwaved for 1-2 minutes. Do not let boil.

Clam Chowder

My dad loves to tinker with recipes. He is known for making a dish repeatedly until it suits him. Clam chowder is on the short list of dishes that he has cooked to death along with pasta alfredo, spare ribs, and brined turkeys. This is my own version.

¾ stick of butter
1 large onion, chopped
2 stalks celery, diced
3 carrots, diced
3 potatoes, diced
3 sprigs fresh thyme
1 teaspoon salt
½ teaspoon pepper
3 cups clam juice
¼ cup flour
2 cups milk
1 (6-8 ounce) can chopped clams, drained

Melt half the butter in a large pot over medium heat. Add onions and sauté for 3-4 minutes. Add celery and thyme. Continue cooking for another 8-10 minutes until vegetables are softened. Add clam juice, potatoes, and carrots. Simmer for 15 to 20 minutes or until potatoes are cooked through.

In a separate pan melt remaining butter and whisk in flour. Continue whisking for 1-2 minutes to make sure the raw flour is cooked a bit. Add a cup or so of hot broth to flour mixture and then whisk everything back into large pot of hot liquid. Cook until thickened. Add in the milk and clams. Leave on low for a couple of minutes or until clams are cooked through. Serve with crackers or toasted ciabatta bread.

*For a richer soup substitute cream for the milk and omit the flour.

Venison Stew

Shoulder cuts work well for this slow roasted venison stew. This is best served over rice with turmeric on page 178.

3-4 pound stew meat (bone-in, if available)
1 large onion, peeled and sliced
4-5 carrots, peeled and cut into 2 inch pieces
3 stalks celery, cut into 2 inch pieces
1 (28 ounce) can whole peeled tomatoes
1 (15 ounce) chick peas, drained and rinsed
1 large zucchini, cut into a large dice
2 large potatoes, peeled and cubed
kosher salt
freshly ground black pepper
fresh thyme
olive oil

Season meat on all sides with salt and pepper. Heat a large Dutch oven over medium heat and add a bit of olive oil and the seasoned meat. Brown meat on both sides, try not to turn or flip the meat too much.

Add the onions and celery, stir to combine. Carefully hand crush the tomatoes into the pot. Add a little water (½ - 1 cup) if necessary and season with a couple teaspoons of thyme, a bit more salt, and pepper. Bring to a boil and then reduce heat and simmer for 2 hours or until meat is tender and can be pulled apart easily.

Add carrots and potatoes and simmer for another 20-30 minutes. Finally, add the can of chick peas and the zucchini and simmer until tender, about 10 minutes.

*If using bone-in stew meat, remove the meat before adding the vegetables. Discard the bones and return the meat to the stew. Simmer with the vegetables and then serve over rice.

*This method would work well for beef or lamb as well.

Pheasant Stew

This recipe started out as a chicken stew recipe, but I found that it is an ideal way to eat pheasant as well. I love to serve this with hearty crackers and a crisp salad. Make your own stock from the carcass if you have time and you'll notice it enhances the flavor tremendously. Feel free to substitute other foul such as quail or turkey, or simply use chicken.

4 whole pheasant breasts, bone in, skin on
3 tablespoons olive oil
5 cups chicken stock
2 chicken bouillon cubes
½ stick unsalted butter
1 onion, diced
¾ cup flour
¼ cup heavy cream
2 cups carrots, diced
2 cups frozen peas
½ cup fresh parsley
2 potatoes, peeled and cubed
kosher salt
freshly ground black pepper

Preheat the oven to 375°F. Place the pheasant breasts on a sheet pan and rub them with olive oil. Sprinkle generously with salt and pepper. Roast for 25 to 30 minutes, or until cooked through. Set aside and cool enough to handle, then remove them from the bones and discard the skin. Cut the pheasant into large dice. You should have 2-3 cups of cubed pheasant.

In a small saucepan, heat the chicken stock and dissolve the bouillon cubes in the stock. In a large pot or Dutch oven, melt the butter and sauté the onions over medium-low heat for 10 to 15 minutes, or until translucent. Add the flour and cook over low heat, stirring constantly for 2 minutes. Add the hot stock to the sauce. Simmer over low heat for 1 more minute, stirring, until thick. Add 2 teaspoons salt, ½ teaspoon pepper, and the heavy cream. Add carrots and potatoes, simmer over medium-low heat for 15 minutes or until tender. Add the pheasant meat, peas, and fresh parsley. Mix well.

At this point I leave it on the lowest setting and allow the flavors to develop until it is time to eat. Serve with biscuits.

* Save the pheasant carcass and make your own pheasant stock. Stock can be frozen and later defrosted in the fridge the next time you make pheasant stew.

Venison Chili

We serve beef chili at the ranch daily because beef is readily available year round, but this venison chili is one of our favorite ways to enjoy our ground Venison during the fall and winter months.

1 pound ground venison
1 onion, diced
3 stalks celery, thinly sliced
1 teaspoon chili powder
½ teaspoon smoked paprika
½ teaspoon cumin
½ teaspoon oregano
½ teaspoon dry garlic
1 (48 ounce) can tomato juice
1 can medium chili beans
1 can kidney beans
red pepper flakes
kosher salt
freshly ground black pepper

Heat a tablespoon of oil in a large pot and add the venison, onion, and celery. Sauté until meat is browned and vegetables are tender. Add spices, a pinch of red pepper flakes, and cook 1 minute more. Add all remaining ingredients and bring up to a boil. Reduce to a simmer for at least 1 hour.

Lentil Soup

We love this hearty soup. It tastes even better the following day and reheats well. This is also a terrific dish to take to a pot luck.

2 tablespoons olive oil
1 tablespoon bacon fat (optional)
1 medium onion, chopped
4 carrots, peeled and chopped
3 celery stalks, chopped
2 garlic cloves, chopped
1 (14 ½ ounce) can whole peeled tomatoes
1 ¼ cups lentils
6-8 cups chicken broth (or water)
kosher salt
freshly ground black pepper
4 sprigs thyme
Parmesan cheese and rind

Heat the oil and bacon fat in a large heavy pot over medium heat. Add onion, carrots, and celery and sauté until tender. Add garlic, salt, and pepper and sauté 2 minutes more. Add the cheese rind and then crush tomatoes with your hands. Add to pot with the juices. Simmer until the juices evaporate a little and the tomatoes start to break down.

Stir in the lentils and mix to coat. Add the thyme and broth (or water) and stir. Bring to a boil over high heat. Cover and simmer over low heat until the lentils are almost tender, about 30-40 minutes. Remove cheese rind.

Ladle the soup into bowls. Sprinkle with Parmesan cheese, drizzle with olive oil, and serve.

Singed

For a portion of my childhood my mom was gone a lot. She spent our early years being a stay at home mom, but once we were in school all day she decided it was time for her to change careers. She enrolled at the nearest university and began pursuing a degree in Elementary Education. To complete her degree she was required to take a few evening classes. It was challenging for her since these classes were over an hour drive from our house in the country.

On those nights my brothers and I had to rely on my father to cook dinner. My father is a good cook, but he is not exactly the finest of caretakers. He ate when he was hungry and left the rest of us to fend for ourselves. We often heated up frozen pot pies, fried up bologna sandwiches, or boiled hot dogs on the days that he was left in charge.

So we were surprised one afternoon when Dad decided that he was actually going to grill something for dinner. He told my older brother, Matt, to get the grill heated and ready. In those days we cooked on a built-in grill on the back patio of our home. The grill was built into a thick brick wall and it had a heavy iron door that opened to the heating element and the propane tank was stored in an underneath compartment.

My older brother, with us in tow, turned the gas on and then left in search of matches. The matches were stored in an upper cabinet in our kitchen My brother pulled a chair close to the cabinet and climbed on top of it. He reached up and felt around with his fingers, searching for the matches. My younger brother and I stood and waited for him, keeping an eye on the grill. When he finally came back he held the box of matches. He fumbled with them for a minute before he was able to get a match out of the box. Just as he struck the match a plume of fire erupted from the grill. My little brother and I watched in horror as my older brother was engulfed in flames. The ball of fire came blasting out of the front and top of the grill and it disappeared almost instantly. The most amazing thing was my brother was unharmed except for the fact that he singed off his eyebrows, eyelashes, and the hair from his arms.

The smell of burning hair filled the air as we all went running into the house. We chased after my brother as he went in search of his snorkel and mask. Once he found them he went racing towards the bathroom and we watched him fill the sink with cold water. He quickly put the mask and snorkel on and plunged his face into the cold water.

Later that night my little brother raced down the driveway to meet my mother as she drove in. He excitedly yelled through the window of the car to Mom, "Matt burned his face off!" I don't remember her reaction or anything else from that night including what we ate for dinner, but I will never forget the look on my brother's face at that terrible moment or seeing him snorkel in the bathroom sink.

Chapter 3 ✳ Salads

My mother planted a very large garden when we were growing up. I looked forward to planting it with her every spring. We would pick out seeds and sow rows and rows of lettuce and a huge variety of vegetables. My favorite task was pollinating the rows of corn. We would shake the tassels and watch the pollen fall like snow.

We serve a number of classic salads at the ranch on a weekly basis. The potato and macaroni salads are standards and they have been served fresh since the very beginning. The potato salad recipe comes from my grandmother, Della, the most loving and spirited person I know.

Classic Potato Salad

Russet potatoes are what we generally use for this dish. Other varieties can be substituted depending on what you prefer.

5 pounds potatoes, peeled and quartered
6 hard boiled eggs
2-3 stalks celery, chopped
¼ cup red pepper
¼ cup green pepper
¼ cup onion, diced
¼ cup sweet relish
1 cup Miracle Whip
1 tablespoon sugar
2 tablespoons mustard
½ teaspoon salt
¼ teaspoon pepper
½ teaspoon celery seeds (optional)

Bring potatoes up to a boil in a large pot of salted water and cook for 10-15 minutes or until fork tender. Drain and let cool completely, this step may be done ahead of time. Combine all remaining ingredients in a large bowl and mix thoroughly. Cube potatoes and add to mixture. Mix gently and refrigerate for at least 2 hours before serving to let the flavors develop. Taste and season again with salt and pepper before serving.

Macaroni Salad

Macaroni salad is another staple served at the ranch. It pairs well with hamburgers, grilled chicken, or a simple sandwich. It can be prepared ahead of time as it keeps well in the refrigerator for up to 4 days.

1 pound elbow noodles
4-5 hard boiled eggs, peeled and chopped
½ cup celery, thinly sliced
1 cup red pepper, diced
½ cup red onion, diced
¾ cup frozen peas
1-2 cups Miracle Whip
kosher salt
freshly ground black pepper

Cook pasta according to box directions, let cool completely. In a large bowl combine celery, red pepper, red onion, peas, 1 cup Miracle Whip, salt, and pepper. Use a large spoon to mix completely. Add cooled pasta and chopped eggs. Mix gently and add additional Miracle Whip if necessary. Refrigerate at least 2 hours before serving to let the flavors develop. Taste and season again with salt and pepper before serving.

*The pasta will absorb the Miracle Whip over time. Mix in a dollop of Miracle Whip to freshen it up.

Crunchy Asian Chopped Salad

This fresh and crunchy salad is the perfect dish to serve at a barbeque or potluck. It is fresh, flavorful, and always a hit.

2 pounds Napa cabbage*
6 strips crispy bacon
⅓ cup slivered almonds, toasted
4 green onions, sliced thinly
¼ cup red onion, diced
½ red pepper, sliced thinly
1 package ramen noodles (with chicken flavoring)
2 tablespoons butter

sauce
½ cup olive oil
¼ cup sugar
2 tablespoons vinegar
2 tablespoons soy sauce
¼ teaspoon pepper

Crush ramen noodles and shred lettuce. In a small sauté pan, melt butter. Add chicken flavoring, ramen noodles, and slivered almonds. Toast over medium to low heat until browned and crisp. Remove and let cool. Mix all salad ingredients in a large bowl. Combine sauce ingredients in a small bowl and whisk together. Pour over salad and toss. Transfer to a clean bowl and serve immediately.

*Romaine lettuce may be substituted.

Broccoli Salad

This salad has it all. It has a bit of sweet, tangy, crunchy, and chewy in every bite. It is the perfect dish to take to a potluck since it can be dressed ahead of time and it remains crisper than a typical salad.

1 large head broccoli
½ cup crumbled bacon
½ cup red onion, chopped
½ cup dried cranberries or raisins
½ cup cashews
1 cup mayonnaise
2 tablespoons white vinegar
¼ cup sugar
½ teaspoon kosher salt
¼ teaspoon freshly ground black pepper

Toast cashews in a small nonstick pan over medium heat until lightly browned, remove and let cool. Wash broccoli thoroughly and cut florets into bite-sized pieces. Place in a colander to dry for a few minutes. Pat dry with paper towels if necessary. In a large bowl combine mayonnaise, vinegar, sugar, salt, and pepper. Whisk until smooth. Add all remaining ingredients and stir to coat with dressing.

Taco Salad

We make taco salad quite often during the summer months. It goes well with burgers, chicken, or hot dogs and looks so bright and happy at any buffet-style event. Be sure to hold off dressing it or adding the Doritos until the very last second because everything will become soggy quickly.

1 head iceberg lettuce
½ pound ground beef
1 cup red kidney beans
1 package taco seasonings
⅓ cup red pepper, diced
⅓ cup red onion, diced
1 tomato, diced
¾ cup shredded cheddar cheese
1 ½ cups crushed Doritos
Western or Catalina dressing

Brown ground beef in a large pan. Add seasoning packet according to directions. Drain beef and cool completely. Tear iceberg lettuce into bite sized pieces and place in a large mixing bowl. Add all remaining ingredients and toss with enough Western dressing to coat. Transfer to clean bowl and serve immediately.

Cowboy Caviar

This is a terrific stand alone salad, but if you try it with tortilla chips you'll find it makes an amazingly good salsa. I always make a huge bowl and let people eat it however they wish, I prefer it with the chips!

½ bag frozen corn
1 (15 ounce) black beans, drained and rinsed
½ red onion, chopped
1 jalapeño pepper, minced
1 avocado, diced
1 lime
cilantro
1 teaspoon chili pepper
1 teaspoon cumin
salt

Mix everything together in a large bowl. Stir to combine. Add more seasoning, depending on your taste. Try to make at least 2 hours before serving so that the flavors have time to develop. Without the avocado, this will easily keep in the refrigerator for up to 4 days.

*If making ahead do not add the avocado until just before serving.

Wilted Spinach Salad

My dad used to make this salad when I was growing up, and I always liked the combination of the dressing, eggs, and bacon. It is a delicious mix of sweet and savory flavors.

4 cups baby spinach, washed
¼ red onion, thinly sliced
1 cup sliced mushrooms
4-5 slices bacon
2 hard boiled eggs, chilled, peeled, and sliced

dressing

¼ cup bacon drippings
¼ cup red wine vinegar
2 teaspoons Dijon mustard
2-3 teaspoons sugar

Fry bacon until browned and crisp. Drain on paper towel-lined plate, reserve drippings. Place spinach, red onion, mushrooms, eggs, and crumbled bacon in a large bowl.

Leave ¼ cup hot bacon drippings in the pan and discard remainder or save for another day. Add red wine vinegar, Dijon mustard, and sugar. Whisk to combine and then pour hot dressing over salad. Toss and enjoy immediately.

Salad in a Jar

These individual salads can be made ahead of time and eaten throughout the work week. They are portable and you can easily tote them to work or pack them in a cooler during the summer months for an easy picnic dish. Planning ahead makes eating healthy much easier.

Pick your favorite ingredients from the list below and layer them in a mason jar to create your favorite salad. My personal favorite way is to layer kidney beans, onion, red pepper, cucumber, and a combination of lettuces. I place a peeled hard boiled egg on top and put the lid on. When it is time to eat I dice the egg into my salad bowl and then dump the rest of the ingredients on top. I add ranch dressing and toss to coat and finish it off with a handful of chow mein noodles.

mixed lettuces
cucumber
tomato
carrot
red or green pepper
green onion or red onion
beans, kidney or pinto
bacon
ham
cold grilled chicken
hard boiled eggs, peeled
feta cheese

Layer your favorite salad ingredients by placing the wettest ingredients toward the bottom of each jar and the mixed lettuces on top. If you are using hard boiled eggs or cheese, place those on the very top. It is best to use a wide mouth canning jar so you can easily get everything in and out. When you are ready to eat just dump your salad onto a salad plate and top with your favorite dressing, croutons, or chow mein noodles and enjoy.

*You can easily make 4-5 of these at a time as they keep well as long as the lettuce is not too wet. I like to pat the lettuce dry with a paper towel if I am making enough for the week.

Hooked

As kids, my brothers and I spent a lot of time exploring the land that was all around us. For a short time our front yard was a wheat field and our backyard was surrounded by swampland and forest. In the summer we would chase grasshoppers and catch frogs. We would swim in the pond and wiggle our toes, waiting for the sunfish to find them and squeal with delight as they began nibbling them. I spent hours collecting wildflowers to give to my mother. Other times I would press them between the pages of a book, saving them for an upcoming 4-H project. In the winter we had fun ice skating on the pond or pulling sleds through the snow with the 3-wheeler. In late winter I enjoyed visiting the neighbors to watch as they tapped trees and made their own maple syrup. They even had a real sugar shack.

While we behaved well most of the time, there were 3 of us, and we happened to get into a lot of mischief. We had bb guns, sling shots, and hatchets. I'm actually quite surprised that all three of us survived with all of our fingers and toes intact. Looking back I have to believe there was supervision and the fact that my mother is the most chronic worrier I have ever met assures me that she knew our whereabouts; but at that age I felt quite certain that we had free reign once our chores were finished.

I remember one summer day when I was quite young, my brother and I were fishing in a small pond my dad had dug behind the clothesline in our backyard. My brother who was 5 or 6 at the time had a long fishing pole and we were taking turns dropping the line in the little pond and reeling up sunfish. We started catching them quite rapidly, and in an effort to maximize our catch I would unhook them and toss them back in while my little brother held the pole. Our system was working well until Nick got a little too anxious and tried to cast while I was still unhooking his last fish. Just as he flicked the line, the hook slipped and went right into the pad of my right thumb.

I remember hollering over and over for my mom to come help, but we were so far away that she could not possibly hear me. After a moment or two, we trudged back through the grass toward the house. We had to walk in tandem because my thumb was still connected to the hook, as well as the floppy fish and the fishing pole.

Once we came into view my mother looked to see what we were doing, and her eyes grew big as she made sense of the situation. She let out a squeal and came rushing over to help. She quickly cut the line and promptly hauled me to the the nearest neighbor, who happened to be a nurse. Judy and her husband assessed the situation and decided the best course of action would be to push the hook through my thumb and out the other side since the hook had a barb that prevented it from going back the way it came.

They left me standing there in their kitchen for a few minutes while they went to search for pliers. Once they came back, mom and Jim held onto my arm so that I wouldn't flinch while Judy pushed the fish hook through my flesh. I probably don't have to tell you this, but I have been a little wary around fishhooks ever since.

Running the Dogs

Dogs are a big aspect of the pheasant hunting business. Trained hunting dogs are quintessential to bird hunting and many types of dogs are required. Some people like a fast paced hunt and prefer dogs that flush the birds and are on the go the whole hunt. Other hunters prefer to pace their hunt and enjoy pointers because they can take their time and prepare for the shot.

As a full service preserve we have always maintained a variety of hunting dogs and guides so that people have options for their hunts. In the early years we had a small kennel with 6 or 7 runs for our personal dogs. As the business grew, we were able to build a larger kennel three times the size of our original kennel, housing personal dogs as well as offering kennel services to clients.

During the season our dogs spend a lot of time hunting the fields and they are kept active, lean, and muscled. However, from mid-April through August it is the off-season so the dogs are no longer hunting everyday. In need of exercise and recreation my dad would give my brothers the job of running the dogs.

"Running the dogs" meant that one of my brothers had to hop on a 3-wheeler and let out the dogs; at times we had up to 10 dogs to run. To keep the dogs lean and fit my brothers would drive miles and miles on the 3-wheeler with the dogs chasing after them the whole time.

From time to time I would ride along and watch the dogs run. One day I went along for a ride when we only had a couple of dogs running, and we started driving down the dirt road in front of our house. We went a couple of miles and wound up going through a bit of a swampy patch. Before we knew it we had gotten our 3-wheeler stuck. Not wanting to get into any trouble my brothers and I took turns trying to push the 3-wheeler loose. Each time we would push the throttle, the back wheels of the 3-wheeler would spin furiously and shoot out thick black muck. Whoever happened to be pushing got covered from head to toe while the driver got residual muck that flung up onto his back and head. By the time we got the 3-wheeler loose we were completely covered in thick black muck. We looked at each other and knew that we had to do a bit of damage control. It was going to be a bit tricky to hide the fact that we had gotten the 3-wheeler stuck now that we were filthy. We also knew that my mom would be one unhappy lady if she saw how black our clothes were.

Once we got loose we hopped on the 3-wheeler and started for home. We drove through the fields and headed through the woods and around the house to our backyard to avoid being seen. Just as we came around the last corner we spotted the pond in our backyard and without even saying a word, we all hopped off the 3-wheeler and jumped in the deep end with all of our clothes on and paddled around until we were clean. We sprayed down the 3-wheeler and parked it as usual.

We ducked into the garage and stripped down to our underwear and threw our wet clothes in the laundry room on the way to our rooms. After we were cleaned and dressed we came back outside and headed towards the kennels. Just as we crossed the driveway, we saw my father storming towards us. We were confused about what he could be angry about since we thought we had ourselves covered. What we had forgotten, in our haste to hide our dirty clothes and the 3-wheeler, was that we had not kenneled the dogs. We had left the two labradors and a large wirehair out roaming around, and they were running around the pheasant pens scaring the birds.

Dad began lecturing us on how irresponsible we had been, and we stood there hanging our heads and looking at the ground. Just as he went into a tirade, the big wirehair, Oscar, came trotting by and paused for a moment next to my dad. The three of us lifted our heads just in time to see Oscar lift his leg and pee down the side of my dad's left leg. He did not even notice what had happened until we burst out laughing. He looked down at his dripping pant-leg and stalked off, leaving us there cackling.

Chapter 4 ✳ Fish

The pressure is on to catch fish when a shore lunch is on the menu. We have to catch fish or settle on eating canned beans for lunch. There have been quite a few fishing trips when we've fished all morning without much more than a bite. It never fails though, just as we start getting nervous we find a hot spot. One year my son was the first to catch a fish for lunch, and he was one proud and excited little fisherman.

Pan Fried Walleye

We have a favorite Canadian fly in fishing outfit that we have vacationed with for years. We always make sure to plan a couple of shore lunches during our week long stay. They are one of the many highlights of the trip.

3-4 fillets per person
1-2 cups dredging flour* (we use Duck's brand)
1 egg
kosher salt
freshly ground black pepper
1 quart vegetable oil
lemon wedges

Fill a frying pan with two inches of oil, heat over medium heat. Whisk the egg and a couple tablespoons of water in a shallow bowl. Place dredging flour and a teaspoon of salt and ½ teaspoon of pepper in a large zip top bag. Dip 3-4 fillets into egg wash and then place in the bag. Shake and then remove filets and fry until golden. Repeat with remaining fish, being careful not to overcrowd the pan.

*Make your own dredging flour by mixing 1 cup flour, ½ cup cornmeal, 1 teaspoon salt, ½ teaspoon pepper, and ½ teaspoon paprika.

Fish Packets with Spinach and Leeks

serves 4

These fish packets can be made with any firm, mild white fish. I have cooked them in an oven, on a grill, and even in the rain over a campfire, and they always turn out incredible.

4 cod fillets
1 leek
1 handful of spinach per packet
½ red bell pepper, thinly sliced
olive oil
kosher salt
freshly ground black pepper

Place 4 large pieces of foil on the counter. Tear a handful of spinach leaves apart and place in the center of each piece of foil. Wash and thinly slice the bottom, white part of the leek and add a quarter of the leek to each packet. Place the bell pepper slices on top of the leeks, reserving two to three for the top of each fish fillet.

Drizzle vegetables with a small amount of oil and season with salt and pepper. Place one fillet on top of each packet and place the remaining peppers on top of each piece of fish. Drizzle with a little more oil and season lightly again.

Pull two sides of foil up over the fish and fold over two times. Fold the open edges over a few times to completely close. Repeat with remaining packets. Place on a sheet pan and bake at 375°F for about 10 minutes. If the fish is white and firm to the touch it is ready. Serve with a scoop of rice.

Fish Tacos

I love a good fish taco and these really hit the spot. You can use practically any mild tasting fish or shrimp in this marinade. The mango salsa makes it something extra special.

1 ½ pounds mild white fish
1 light beer
1 lime
¼ cup apple or orange juice

mango salsa

1 large ripe mango, peeled and cubed
½ red pepper, diced
¼ cup diced red onion
1 tablespoon fresh jalapeño, minced
cilantro
lime juice
salt

Mix the light beer, juice of 1 lime, and apple juice in a shallow baking dish. Place fillets in the marinade and refrigerate for 20-30 minutes. Mix remaining ingredients in a medium bowl. Set aside. Heat grill, remove fish from marinade and season with salt and pepper. Grill for 3 minutes per side or until fish is opaque and flakes easily. Warm tortillas, assemble tacos, and enjoy.

Salmon with a Sweet Soy Sauce Glaze

This quick and easy salmon is a crowd pleaser and special enough to impress guests. It only take a few minutes to prep and then you can pop it in the oven minutes before eating.

Try the crusted salmon on the following page for another variation. I often prepare both recipes and let guests choose between them or try both if they feel inclined. This goes well with green beans, fresh asparagus, or a light salad.

1 whole salmon filet
2 cloves garlic, minced
1 teaspoon ginger
⅓ cup soy sauce
2 tablespoons brown sugar
1 tablespoon honey

Whisk marinade in a medium bowl. Place fish in a large zip top bag and cover with ⅔ of the marinade. Refrigerate for at least 2 hours and up to 6 hours.

Preheat oven to 400°F. Remove fish from marinade and place on a foil lined sheet pan. Bake in preheated oven for 20 minutes, basting at least twice with reserved marinade. Remove when the flesh of the fish feels firm to the touch and flakes when cut.

*Portion salmon prior to cooking for a fancier presentation.

Crusted Salmon with Honey Mustard Glaze

This is my favorite way to prepare salmon. I love the sweet and spicy glaze as well as the crispy crust. I like to make a little extra honey mustard sauce and serve it on the side in case anyone would like a little more.

1 whole salmon filet
½ cup Panko breadcrumbs
3 tablespoons melted butter
2 tablespoons Dijon mustard
2 tablespoons honey
1 tablespoon parsley, chopped
kosher salt
freshly ground black pepper

Whisk the Dijon mustard and honey together in a medium bowl. Place the salmon filet on a foil lined sheet pan and spoon over the honey mustard glaze making sure to coat the entire fillet. Mix the breadcrumbs, butter, parsley, salt, and pepper in a second bowl. Sprinkle evenly over the top of the fish. Drizzle with a touch more melted butter or olive oil.

Preheat oven to 400°F. Bake in heated oven for 20 minutes. Remove when the flesh of the fish feels firm to the touch and flakes when cut.

*Standard breadcrumbs can be substituted for the Panko.

Salmon Dip

Leftover baked salmon can be transformed into this appetizer. It is best served with multigrain crackers and a crisp glass of wine.

1 baked salmon filet*, skin removed and flaked
1 (8 ounce) package cream cheese, softened
¼ cup red onion, chopped
4 scallions, chopped
2 teaspoons fresh dill, minced
a pinch of salt
freshly ground black pepper
olive oil

Heat a tablespoon of olive oil in a small pan and sauté the red onions until soft. In a stand mixer, whip the cream cheese until smooth and set aside. Stir cooked onions into the cream cheese mixture. Add all remaining ingredients except salmon and mix well. Carefully fold in the flaked salmon. Serve with crackers.

*Bake your salmon with a drizzle of olive oil, salt, and pepper for 15-20 minutes at 350° F or until salmon flakes easily with a fork. Cool completely before using in this recipe.

Salmon Patties with Creamed Pea Sauce

makes 8 cakes

One day I was half watching a cooking show on PBS while I was making dinner and suddenly my son shouted from the living room "Mom, you should make that!" I turned to look and saw the host cutting up fresh salmon and forming it into cakes. Weeks went by and I forgot about the salmon cakes until we were grocery shopping one day and my son saw fresh salmon in the fish case and begged me to make the salmon cakes he saw on television. This is what I came up with and he was pretty pleased!

1 pound fresh salmon, skin removed
1 cup plus 3 tablespoons Panko or breadcrumbs, divided
1 green onion, thinly sliced
1 tablespoon onion, minced
2 tablespoons fresh parsley, minced
2 tablespoons mayonnaise
2 tablespoons lemon juice
1 teaspoon Dijon mustard
¾ teaspoon salt
¼ teaspoon pepper
¼ teaspoon smoked paprika
olive oil

Combine all ingredients except Panko and salmon in a large bowl. Chop the salmon into small pieces, about ¼ inch or smaller and add to mixture. Mix thoroughly and shape ⅓ cup of the mixture into cakes and coat in Panko (or breadcrumbs.) Repeat with remaining salmon mixture.

Heat 2-3 tablespoons of olive oil in a large skillet over medium heat. Cook salmon cakes until golden brown on both sides. Remove to a paper towel-lined plate.

Creamed Pea Sauce

4 tablespoons butter
4 tablespoons flour
1 teaspoon salt
½ teaspoon pepper
2 ½ cups half and half
1 cup peas (fresh or frozen)

Melt the butter in a medium saucepan. Whisk in the flour and seasonings.
Cook for 2-3 minutes. Gradually whisk in the half and half and bring to a
gentle boil. Simmer until the sauce thickens. Add peas and cook 3-4
minutes more. Spoon over salmon cakes.

Vacation

One summer day my dad decided that we needed to upgrade our flight pens, and he ordered my brothers and I to hog ring netting to the chicken wire surrounding the base of the pens. To "hog ring" means we were each given a hand held tool, much like pliers, but with a specialized tip that holds a c-shaped metal link. We placed a link on the tip of the tool and then grabbed a bit of netting and a bit of fence with the link and squeezed tightly to pinch the c-shaped link closed. It was the perfect job for us because it was very simple and repetitive. We got very good at it and would race each other to make it more fun.

However, this particular day we did not feel like racing. It happened to be the Fourth of July. A day when every other kid in America was watching a parade somewhere collecting candy and waving their little red, white, and blue flags happily. We were not watching any parades, collecting candy, or waving any flags. We did not get to spend time with our friends enjoying the day. We were, in fact, a bit put out that our dad would make us stand out in the sun on a 100+ degree day "hog ringing" instead of enjoying the day like every other kid we knew. So, fed up with the heat, we dropped our tools and marched up to him as a group and complained about the situation he had put us in. We told him what he was doing to us was not fair and we wouldn't stand for it.

So, dear reader, you won't believe this, but he told us that he would take us on a vacation. We were so excited! This was going to be big! He had us follow him toward the house and then he told us to close our eyes. We obediently closed our eyes and waited anxiously. We could hear him working for a moment and then he told us to open our eyes and take a drink from the garden hose he was holding. Perplexed, we cocked our heads and looked up at him trying to make sense of what he was asking us to do and how it had anything to do with our vacation. He looked down at us and in all seriousness, told us to take a drink and then close our eyes and imagine that we were taking a cool, crisp drink from the drinking fountain on the vacation of our dreams in Disney World. Then he told us our vacation was over and it was time to get back to work.

We were all so incredibly mad. I actually can't remember ever being more upset than I was right then. However, this story is one of my father's favorites to tell from our childhood, and we get to relive it everytime there happens to be a garden hose within his reach. I know he takes pride in the fact that he tricked all three of us at the same time, and he has had fun rubbing it in for over 25 years.

Chapter 5 ✳ Poultry

By nature, pheasant happens to be very lean. Without any fat it becomes tricky to prepare without drying out. Here are a few of our favorite ways to prepare pheasant that turn out delicious savory dishes. Feel free to substitute chicken in any of these recipes or experiment with other foul you may have.

Pheasant with Country Stuffing

This is a very elegant preparation for pheasant that you can serve at a party. It is easy to slice and looks very impressive. Try this with chicken or turkey for another variation.

1 pheasant skin-on, deboned*
butter
prepared stuffing

Prepare stuffing, either Country Apple Stuffing (page 167) or Joy's Sausage Stuffing (page 168) will work for this preparation.

Preheat oven to 400°F. Lay out your deboned pheasant. Spread a 1-inch thick layer of your stuffing mixture onto the inside flesh of the pheasant. Press some of the mixture into the leg cavities. Roll pheasant together, incasing the stuffing, and tie with kitchen twine.

Baste with melted butter and place in oven. Insert a digital thermometer and roast for around 1 hour or until center reads 165°F, basting with butter every 20 minutes.

*You may ask a butcher to debone your chicken, if using, otherwise do an online search for deboning instructions. There is a terrific online video of chef Jacques Pepin preparing a chicken galantine you might like to take a look at.

Pheasant with Marsala and Mushrooms

I based this dish on a chicken dish called Rigatoni D that I've had at Maggiano's, a famous restaurant chain in Chicago. The original version calls for chicken, but pheasant works so well I prefer it now. It stays moist and tender in the cream sauce.

2 tablespoons extra virgin olive oil
1 (10 ounce) package button mushrooms
1 yellow onion, chopped
2 teaspoons garlic, minced
1 pound pheasant breast, cut into 1 inch cubes
2 cups chicken stock
½ cup sweet marsala wine (moscato can be substituted)
¼ cup white wine (optional)
¾ cup heavy cream
1 pound pasta, rigatoni, campanella, or penne
1 tablespoon fresh basil
2 tablespoons parmesan cheese, grated
2 tablespoons butter
kosher salt
freshly ground black pepper
parsley for garnish

Heat oil in a large nonstick pan. Sauté mushrooms and onions until lightly browned. Season with salt and pepper and then add pheasant and garlic. Cook 3-4 minutes or until pheasant begins to brown slightly on the outside, add chicken stock, marsala, and white wine, if using. Bring to a boil and then turn down and simmer until reduced by half. Add cream over low heat until warmed through. Cook pasta according to package directions. Drain and add to pheasant mixture. Finish with basil, Parmesan cheese, butter, salt and pepper. Garnish with parsley and serve.

Pheasant Tenders

Pheasant tenders are a hit with adults as well as kids of all ages. They are so crisp and delicious. Serve with a honey mustard sauce and everyone will be coming back for seconds.

2 pounds pheasant breasts
2 eggs
½ cup buttermilk
1 cup breading* (we use Duck's brand all purpose breading)
oil for frying

Slice pheasant breasts lengthwise to create two long tenders. In one bowl whisk the eggs and buttermilk together. Place breading in another bowl. Dip tenders in milk mixture and then dredge in breading. Heat an inch or two of vegetable oil in a heavy cast iron pan over medium heat. Oil should be hot when you place tenders in pan. Be sure not to overcrowd the pan and fry tenders for 4-5 minutes per side or until crisp on the outside and cooked through. Repeat with remaining tenders.

*Alternate breading: 1 cup Panko or breadcrumbs, 2 tablespoons grated Parmesan, 1 teaspoon kosher salt, and ½ teaspoon freshly ground black pepper

Honey Mustard Dipping Sauce

½ cup honey
¼ cup Dijon mustard
¼ cup mayonnaise

Combine sauce ingredients in a small bowl and serve with pheasant tenders.

Pheasant Stir Fry

We have been making a version of this stir fry for the past 20 years. It is light and healthy, and it is so easy that even my kids can cook this dish.

1 pound pheasant meat, thinly sliced
1 small onion, sliced
1 red pepper, sliced
2 carrots, julienned
1 zucchini, sliced
1 cup broccoli florets
2 eggs
½ cup soy sauce
2 tablespoons toasted sesame seed oil
1 ½ cups rice, cook according to package

Heat 1 tablespoon vegetable oil in a medium skillet. Crack the eggs in the pan and mix briefly to break the yolks. Cook for 1 minute or until set and flip. Cook 1 minute more and transfer to a plate. Add pheasant strips and cook until browned and just cooked through, transfer to plate.

Add onions and cook for 6-7 minutes or until tender. Add red pepper and carrot to pan, cook an additional 3-4 minutes. Add zucchini, broccoli, soy sauce, sesame oil, chicken, and eggs. Stir to coat and cook 3-4 minutes or until zucchini and broccoli are tender. Serve over rice.

*Sugar snap peas and cauliflower also make great additions. If using, add these at the same time as you would normally add the zucchini and broccoli in the recipe.

Pheasant with Onions and Sumac

This dish is a take on a Middle Eastern dish called Musakhan. The onions cook down and caramelize in the pan creating an amazing sauce that can be scooped up with torn bits of warm pita. This is a family favorite in our home.

2 pheasants, skin on
4 onions
¼ cup sumac
1 teaspoon cinnamon
½ teaspoon allspice
½ teaspoon nutmeg
1-2 teaspoons kosher salt
½ teaspoon freshly ground black pepper
¼ cup olive oil, reserved

Cut the pheasant into 4 sections. I section them into two bone-in breast pieces and two leg/thigh sections. Mix all of the ingredients, except the olive oil, together in a large bowl. Use your hands to thoroughly mix and massage the spices into the meat and onions. Cover and marinate for a few hours or overnight in the fridge.

Prepare a large casserole dish with nonstick spray or oil and transfer pheasant mixture to dish. Coat with reserved olive oil, cover with foil, and bake at 350°F for 1 hour. Uncover and cook an additional 30 minutes or until onions are tender and pheasant is cooked through. (Sometimes I broil it at the end for a few minutes to brown if necessary.) Serve with warm pita bread and a crisp salad.

*Sumac can be found in the Middle Eastern section of most grocery stores. It has a bright lemony flavor and pairs well with pheasant and chicken.

Marinated Pheasant Skewers

These pheasant skewers grill up so quickly and taste terrific hot off the grill. If you substitute chicken use boneless/skinless thigh meat for best results. Serve with rice and cucumber yogurt sauce.

2 pounds boneless/skinless pheasant breast or thighs
3 lemons
2 tablespoons olive oil
1 teaspoon kosher salt
½ teaspoon freshly ground black pepper

Cut pheasant breasts and thighs into strips (cut across the grain for a better result) and place in a large zip top bag. Cut lemons in half and squeeze juice onto pheasant. Drizzle with olive oil. Season with salt and pepper. Close zip top bag and flip the bag over while massaging the pheasant mixture to coat completely with marinade. Refrigerate for at least 30 minutes and up to 1 hour. The lemon juice will begin to "cook" the meat if left for much longer.

Remove from refrigerator and thread meat on skewers. Grill 2-3 minutes per side or until cooked through.

Cucumber Yogurt Sauce

1 cup plain yogurt
½ cucumber, peeled and diced
¼ red onion, thinly sliced
½ teaspoon salt and
¼ teaspoon freshly ground black pepper

Combine ingredients in a large bowl and season with salt and pepper. Let rest in refrigerator for at least 30 minutes.

Split Pheasant with Paprika

By removing the back bone and laying the bird flat, it allows for more even cooking which produces a moister bird. Kitchen shears are the best tool for removing the backbone. Serve alongside scalloped potatoes and asparagus for a complete meal.

2 pheasants, skin on
1-2 tablespoons smoked paprika
1 teaspoon kosher salt
½ teaspoon freshly ground black pepper
olive oil

Preheat oven to 375°F. Using kitchen shears, cut down both sides of the backbone, discard bones. Lightly run a knife down the inside breastbone to score the bone. Turn pheasant skin side up and lay on a lined sheet pan. Press down to flatten the bird. Tuck wing tip over top of shoulder to secure.

In a small bowl mix paprika, salt, and pepper. Liberally season all sides of pheasant with spice mixture. Separate skin from breast meat and rub a bit of seasoning under the skin directly on the breast meat. Drizzle skin with olive oil and bake for 40-50 minutes or until meat thermometer reads 160°F. Remove and let rest for 10 minutes before serving.

*For crisper skin place under the broiler for a couple of minutes.

*This recipe also works well for chicken, as pictured, just be sure to add cooking time as chickens are much larger birds.

Asian Lettuce Cups with Pheasant

Lettuce wraps are a light and healthy way to enjoy pheasant or chicken. Make these for a quick and tasty lunch or a light dinner.

1 pound pheasant meat, cubed
1 small onion, sliced thinly
2 large carrots, julienned
1 red pepper, julienned
1 tablespoon rice wine vinegar
3 tablespoons soy sauce
1 tablespoon toasted sesame oil
2 tablespoons honey
1-2 heads Boston lettuce, washed
vegetable oil
chow mein noodles

In a small measuring cup whisk rice wine vinegar, soy sauce, sesame oil, and honey. Set sauce aside.

Cover bottom of skillet with a thin layer of oil. Over medium heat, cook pheasant meat until just cooked through and no pink remains. Remove from pan and set aside. Add a bit more oil to the hot pan and add onions, carrots, and red peppers. Cook over medium heat until tender. Return pheasant to pan. Drizzle sauce over mixture, stir to coat. Serve with Boston lettuce cups. Top with chow mein noodles, if desired.

*If you like a thicker sauce, whisk 2 teaspoons of cornstarch into the sauce mixture before cooking.

Pheasant and Bacon Wraps

The pheasant in this recipe can be replaced with chicken, thin cuts of steak, bison, elk, venison, or pork. It can also be grilled or broiled so it is really quite versatile.

1-2 pounds pheasant breast
4 jalapeños
1 red pepper
1-2 packages cream cheese or Boursin cheese
1 pound thick cut premium bacon
1 bottle Italian dressing
kosher salt
freshly ground black pepper

Use a meat mallet to gently pound out the pheasant breasts. Slice the breast length-wise in half. Spread 1-2 tablespoons of cream cheese in the center of the breast. Lay 2 thin slices of jalapeño pepper and 2 thin slices of red pepper on top of the cream cheese. Sprinkle with salt and pepper.

Wrap a slice of bacon around the pheasant breast mixture and secure each end with a toothpick. Repeat with remaining ingredients. Place in a casserole pan and pour the Italian dressing over the pheasant. Marinate at least 1 hour or overnight. Grill or broil until bacon is crisp and pheasant is cooked through.

Pheasant and Vegetable Pasta

This dish is loosely based on a dish I had at Olive Garden years and years ago. It is no longer on the menu, but it was a favorite of mine. This pheasant version is delicious.

1 pound pasta (penne, bowtie, fusilli or campanella)
1 pound pheasant meat, thinly sliced
1 zucchini, sliced
1 small red onion, thinly sliced
1 red pepper, thinly sliced
1 cup fresh asparagus, cut into 2-inch pieces
1 cup peas
2 cloves garlic, minced
5 sprigs fresh thyme
kosher salt
freshly ground black pepper
1 teaspoon dried bouquet garni or herbs de Provence

sauce
1 ½ cups chicken stock
½ cup half and half or cream
½ cup Parmesan cheese
3 tablespoons butter
¼ cup fresh lemon juice

Cook pasta according to box directions. While pasta is cooking, season pheasant with herb mixture, salt, pepper, and thyme. Heat vegetable oil and brown pheasant in medium pan. Add garlic during the last minute of cooking to prevent burning. Remove pheasant, add onions and cook over medium heat for 3-4 minutes or until slightly tender. Add remaining vegetables except the peas. Add chicken stock and simmer for 5 minutes, or until tender.

Stir in remaining sauce ingredients along with peas. Fold in the chicken and pasta. Serve with extra Parmesan cheese.

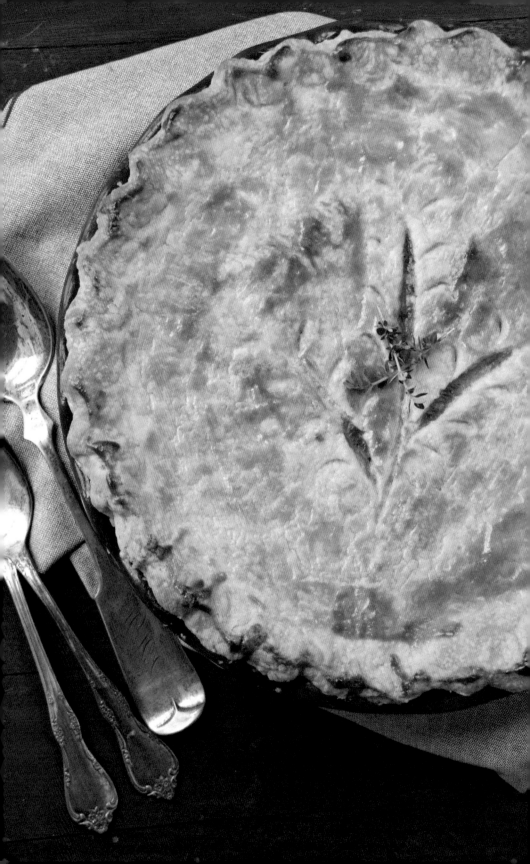

Pheasant Pot Pie

Pot pie is such a homey meal. I can definitely imagine curling up on the couch with a warm blanket and tucking into a big bowlful of this pot pie. This pheasant version is a delicious way to use your wild game. You could also substitute turkey, venison or beef for some variety.

3-4 whole pheasant breasts, bone in, skin on
½ stick unsalted butter
1 small onion, diced
½ cup celery, thinly sliced
2 cups carrots diced
2 potatoes, peeled and cubed
⅔ cup flour
4 cups chicken stock*
¼ cup heavy cream or milk
1 cup frozen peas
1 teaspoon fresh thyme
3 tablespoons olive oil
kosher salt
freshly ground black pepper

Preheat the oven to 375°F. Place the pheasant breasts on a sheet pan and rub them with olive oil. Sprinkle generously with salt and pepper. Roast for 20 to 25 minutes, or until cooked through. Set aside and cool enough to handle, then remove the bones and discard the skin. Cut the pheasant meat into bite-sized pieces.

Heat the chicken stock in a small saucepan. In a large pot or Dutch oven, melt the butter and sauté the onions and celery over medium-low heat for 10 minutes, or until translucent. Add the flour and cook over low heat, stirring constantly for 2 minutes. Add the hot chicken stock to the sauce. Simmer over low heat for 1 more minute, stirring until thick. Add 2 teaspoons salt, ½ teaspoon pepper, and the heavy cream. Add carrots and potatoes, simmer over medium-low for 15 minutes or until tender. Add the chicken, peas, and thyme. Mix well.

*You may substitute 4 cups water and 2 bouillon cubes for the chicken stock if necessary.

*If your filling does not seem quite thick enough whisk ½ cup milk, ¼ cup flour, and ¼ cup hot stock together and slowly whisk into filling a bit at a time until it thickens up. You may not need to add all of the mixture.

Crust

3 cups flour
1 teaspoon salt
1 cup vegetable shortening
9-10 tablespoons ice cold water

Using a pastry cutter combine the flour, salt, and shortening until the largest pieces resemble small peas. With a fork, stir in one tablespoon of water at a time until the mixture clumps together when squeezed gently. Divide and form into two discs and chill for at least 30 minutes.

Remove from refrigerator and roll out first disc and place in bottom of 9 inch pie pan. Roll out remaining dough into a large enough circle to cover the pie plate. Add pheasant filling. Roll top crust around rolling pin and carefully unroll over filling. Use a knife to cut 3-4 vents and trim edges. Crimp edges with your fingers or a fork. Brush top with egg yolk, if desired. Bake in a 375°F oven for 45-60 minutes or until crust is golden brown and crisp.

Field Dressing

Opening day of deer season is a big day around our house. All of the men gather before dawn for breakfast, and then they get themselves dressed and head out to their hunting blinds. My mom and I normally stayed home listening intently all morning for gun shots. We would try to guess what direction the shots came from and whether or not they had a hit or miss. Then we would wait for the men to come back throughout the day. I always enjoyed this because I would get the inside scoop on who got what and when.

From time to time, my dad would invite me to sit with him in the field. I also enjoyed being in the forest so I would bundle up and head out with him while the sun was rising. First, we would quietly walk out toward the blind. If there was snowfall, I would make a game out of trying to step directly in my dad's footsteps the whole way so we would only leave one set of tracks. More often than not, my dad would turn to me at some point and whisper for me to freeze or get down. Sometimes he would see or hear a deer, and he would direct me to crawl. As a kid I found this quite interesting, and I always imagined that I was a Native American hunter stalking my prey or that I was the boy from *My Side of the Mountain* living off the land.

Once we got to the blind we would sit quietly and use our hands to point out deer, woodpeckers, raccoons, or any other animals we might happen to see. We would watch herds of doe come in and out and wait patiently for a buck to appear. We'd pass up most of them and wait for one large enough to be a trophy to come walking by. Once Dad raised up his gun, I would know he had selected his buck. Sometimes he would offer me the gun, but I'd usually pass and let him take the deer. I'd wait for him to shoot and then we'd watch the deer go down and then wait a bit more. After a few moments we would search for the deer and then field dress it.

I always thought deer hunting was pretty easy because we always had such good luck. I didn't understand men that came back saying they hadn't seen anything or those that had taken a shot at a big buck and had missed because they suffered from "buck fever." I had always watched my dad hunt and never experienced anything like that. We'd usually pass up bucks and have multiple herds make their way through our area.

So it didn't come as any surprise to me when we made it to our blind one year towards the very end of the season and barely had time to sit down before a buck came right down our lane. It was a monster 10-pointer, and Dad handed the gun to me and told me to hold steady and wait for the buck to get a bit closer. I waited another minute or two while the buck made his way quietly through the brush, and when Dad gave me the go ahead I pulled the trigger lightly and looked up in time to see the buck jump and disappear into the forest.

I looked up at Dad disappointed and told him I thought I had missed him, but Dad assured me that it had been a direct hit. We waited a few minutes and then we headed into the woods to find my buck. When we came across him I was surprised by my shot, and Dad was super proud that we'd gotten such a nice buck.

I watched as Dad field dressed him. Field dressing didn't bother me since I had dressed thousands of pheasants, but that day Dad had me spear the deer's heart with a branch and carry it back to my mom who would prepare it for dinner. I guess I'd have to say that was my very least favorite part about deer hunting.

Chapter 6 ✳ Meats

Slow roasted meats and stews are a delicious way to serve a hungry group of friends on a cold night. The slow roasted carnitas in this chapter are a good choice when entertaining because all of the work can be done in advance, and you will be free to mingle with your guests.

The slow roasted ribs are also a good choice for a barbeque because you can bake them off the day before or in the morning and throw them on the grill with some extra barbeque sauce just before eating.

The venison recipes are very versatile and work well with beef or other wild game. When making the meatball, meatloaf, or meat pie recipes it is nice to mix in a bit of fattier beef with your ground venison since venison tends to be very lean.

Venison Meatballs

makes about 52 (¾ ounce) meatballs

Venison is a very lean meat so meatballs are a good choice since you can add in a bit of moisture through the addition of vegetables, dairy, and herbs. I like to oven bake the meatballs and let them simmer away in a thick tomato sauce or mushroom gravy until it's time to eat.

1 ½ pounds ground venison (or ¾ pound venison + ¾ pound beef or pork)
2 slices bread, cubed
½ onion, diced
1 egg
¼ cup grated Parmesan cheese
⅓ cup milk
1 teaspoon kosher salt
½ teaspoon freshly ground pepper
2 tablespoons fresh parsley, chopped
1 teaspoon oregano

Mix all ingredients in a large bowl, I find that my hands are the best tool for mixing the meatballs. Use a tablespoon or a small ice cream scoop to form meatballs. Place each meatball on a foil or parchment lined baking sheet. Bake in a 350°F preheated oven for 15-20 minutes.

Mushroom Gravy

For a Polish twist serve these meatballs over boiled potatoes topped with a dollop of grated beets. My friend Eva introduced me to this combination and I think it is quite delicious.

8 ounces sliced mushrooms
1 red or green pepper, diced
1 small onion, diced
1 tablespoon olive oil
⅓ cup flour
1 ½ cups chicken broth
2 teaspoons Hungarian sweet paprika
½ cup heavy cream
½ cup sour cream
fresh parsley
kosher salt
freshly ground black pepper

Heat olive oil over medium heat in a large sauté pan. Add mushrooms, peppers, and onion. Season with salt and pepper and sauté vegetables until they are tender. Sprinkle flour over vegetables and cook 2 more minutes. Slowly whisk in broth and bring up to a boil. Season with additional salt and pepper, if necessary, and add paprika. Continue cooking until mixture thickens. Whisk in heavy cream and sour cream. Add warm meatballs. Remove from heat and stir in fresh parsley.

Venison with Peppers and Onions

My mother used to make this dish, and she always served it with mashed potatoes. It was a favorite of mine growing up. It is another delicious way of preparing venison for loved ones that don't like the gamey taste of venison.

1-2 pounds venison backstrap or round steaks, thinly sliced
1 red pepper, sliced
1 green pepper, sliced
1 large Spanish onion, sliced
¼ cup Worcestershire sauce
1 cup beef or chicken stock
kosher salt
freshly ground black pepper

Heat 2 tablespoons of vegetable oil in a large skillet over medium heat. Season meat with salt and pepper and then add meat to skillet and cook until browned and just cooked through. Remove from pan, add a touch more oil, add onions and sauté 5-10 minutes or until translucent.

Add peppers and season with salt and pepper. Add Worcestershire sauce and stock. Cover and simmer for 6-8 minutes, or until peppers are tender. Return meat to pan. Serve over mashed potatoes.

*If using round steaks it is a good idea to pound your steaks with a meat tenderizer before slicing and browning.

Venison Swiss Steak

As a child I loved gravy. I would eat it by the spoonful when no one was looking. Swiss Steak appealed to me mainly because of the gravy that was created when it cooked. I loved spooning it all over my mashed potatoes.

2 pounds venison round steak
2 medium onions, thinly sliced
½ cup flour
1 cup water or broth
1 ½ cups chicken or beef broth
¼ cup flour
1 tablespoon Worcestershire sauce or soy sauce
vegetable oil
kosher salt
freshly ground black pepper

Preheat oven to 350°F. In a large zip top bag, place ½ cup flour and a teaspoon each of salt and pepper. One at a time, toss steaks in flour mixture and then pound steaks with a meat mallet or the edge of a plate until ¼ to ½ inch thick. Repeat with all remaining steaks and then lightly dust meat with another coating of flour. Heat 2 tablespoons of oil in a heavy pot or Dutch oven and brown steaks on both sides. You may need to do this in batches depending on the size of your pan as you don't want to crowd the meat.

Once all of the meat is browned return it to the pot, add the onions, 1 cup water and Worcestershire (or soy) sauce. Bring up to a boil and then cover and transfer to oven. Cook for 1 ½ hours. Near the end of the cooking time, whisk broth, ¼ cup flour, ½ teaspoon salt, and ½ teaspoon pepper in a small bowl. Transfer meat to cooktop and uncover. Slowly whisk broth mixture into meat and return to oven for an additional 30 minutes. Remove from oven and serve with mashed potatoes or egg noodles.

Venison Stuffed Cabbage

Stuffed cabbage is a great way to serve venison to friends or family that complain about the taste of wild game. The lemon and cabbage are so flavorful that they won't even know they are eating venison. It is also a perfect way to deal with random cuts of meat, just be sure to cut off any silver skin before mincing.

Now to be fair, you should tell your guests before serving them something they might not be okay with, but feel free to trick your kids, we have successfully won over our kids many times by saying they are eating beef or chicken when they are, in fact, eating wild game.

1 large head of cabbage
1 pound minced venison (or ½ pound venison + ½ pound beef or pork)
1 cup rice, washed and drained of water
3 lemons, juiced (2 additional lemons for serving)
2 heads garlic, sliced thinly
1 teaspoon cinnamon
½ teaspoon allspice
½ teaspoon cumin
1 tablespoon olive oil
1 ½ teaspoons salt

Fill a large pot ⅔ of the way with water and bring it to a low boil. Cut the core out of the cabbage and place the entire head of cabbage in the boiling water. Boil for about 5 minutes and then carefully remove each leaf as it loosens. I often use a fork and a pair of tongs to gently peel each leaf off and place it on a sheet pan to cool. Do not try to force the leaves apart or they will tear, simply leave them to boil for another minute or two and then try again.

While cabbage is cooling, mix meat, rice, spices, and ½ teaspoon salt in a bowl. Set aside. Take the cooled cabbage leaves and cut the thickest part of the stem out. Use kitchen shears to cut a V-shape, removing the tough vein out of each leaf. Use the three largest, most outer leaves to line the bottom of the heavy Dutch oven.

Spread 1-2 tablespoons of the meat mixture on the edge of a cabbage leaf (start with the darkest leaves). Roll each leaf, folding the edges over the meat, like a burrito, and line the rolls carefully in the Dutch oven or large pot. Continue until you run out of meat or cabbage. You should end up with 3-4 layers of rolls.

Heat olive oil in a sauté pan and fry garlic until golden brown. Pour over the cabbage rolls. Mix 3½ cups of water with lemon juice and 1 teaspoon of salt. Pour over garlic and cabbage. Carefully rotate pot around to saturate all of the rolls and then bring up to a boil and then reduce to a low simmer for 1½ hours until rice is fully cooked. Also, check occasionally to make sure there is still enough liquid left, do not let it get dry, add a little water if necessary. Serve with lemon wedges.

Venison Meat Pies

Meat pies are my absolute favorite way to eat venison. The meat filling is typically made with minced lamb or beef, so feel free to substitute those in place of Venison. I usually hand cut a pound of chuck roast, but this version is made with ground venison which is tasty although not authentic.

dough

3-3 ½ cups flour
1 cup warm water
1 egg
2 ½ teaspoons rapid rise yeast
2 teaspoons honey
½ teaspoon salt

In the bowl of a stand mixer add warm water, honey, and yeast. Allow to sit for 2-3 minutes, add the egg. Using a dough hook, gradually add 3 cups flour and salt, mixing until dough forms a ball. Be sure to scrape down the sides of the mixing bowl from time to time. Add more flour, if necessary. Dough should be smooth and elastic. Continue mixing dough with dough hook for 4-5 minutes more. Remove dough and divide into 12 equal balls. Place balls on a flour dusted, parchment-lined sheet pan. Dust tops with additional flour and cover with a sheet of plastic wrap followed by a clean towel. Let rise in a warm place for 1 hour, or until doubled in bulk.

filling

1 pound ground venison (or ½ pound venison + ½ pound beef or pork)
4 cloves garlic, minced
1-2 large onions, thinly sliced (about 2 cups)
1 teaspoon cinnamon
½ teaspoon allspice
1 teaspoon cumin
¼ cup slivered almonds or pine nuts
1 teaspoon kosher salt
½ teaspoon ground black pepper
2 tablespoons clarified butter or olive oil

In a large pot add a tablespoon of butter, onions, salt, and pepper. Fry the onions over medium heat until translucent and tender. Add garlic and cook an additional 1 minute. Add ground venison and seasonings, cook until browned. Be sure to break the meat up as it browns.

Taste mixture and adjust seasonings. In a small pan toast almonds in the remaining clarified butter until golden and then add to meat mixture. Allow to cool.

assemble

Place one ball of dough on a floured surface. Using a rolling pin, roll into a thin disc about 6 inches in diameter. Place ¼ cup of the meat mixture onto the center of the disc. Grab the dough at 2 o'clock and 10 o'clock, pull together and crimp the seam. Pull the dough up at 6 o'clock and crimp the bottom seam to completely seal in the meat mixture. Place seam side down on a floured cookie sheet. Repeat with remaining dough. Brush tops with olive oil. Preheat oven to 400°F and place an overturned empty cookie sheet on middle rack. When oven is hot, place meat pies on heated cookie sheet and bake until dough is browned on top, 8-10 minutes.

Venison Meatloaf

This meatloaf turns out juicy and tender. It is best served with mashed potatoes and green beans the first night. Leftovers can be sliced and reheated to make meatloaf sandwiches the second day.

¾ pound ground venison
¾ pound ground pork or beef
2 slices bread, diced
1 egg
½ cup milk
½ small onion, diced
¼ cup parsley, chopped
1 tablespoon yellow mustard
2 tablespoons ketchup
1 teaspoon kosher salt
½ teaspoon freshly ground black pepper

Preheat oven to 350°F and line a sheet pan with foil or parchment paper. Use hands to combine all ingredients in a large bowl. Make sure everything is completely incorporated and then place mixture on sheet pan. Form into a loaf shape. Baking time depends on shape of loaf, but should take about 35-45 minutes or until internal temperate reaches 160°F. Remove from oven and let rest for 5-10 minutes before slicing.

*You can shape the meat into individual meatloaves as well. Reduce baking time accordingly.

*Feel free to mince the onion in a food processor before mixing into the meat mixture. This will give you a smoother texture as well as a moister meatloaf.

Slow Roasted Pork Ribs

My dad used to make horrible country style ribs. He would boil the ribs in pineapple juice and then grill them off with a slathering of barbeque sauce. They were honestly the toughest things I've ever eaten. When I first got married I tried his technique and decided that boiling the meat in pineapple juice didn't actually impart flavor, it stripped the meat of all of it's flavor, and I needed to simmer them much longer than he ever did to make them tender. I didn't care for that method and set out to find a better way to cook ribs. At the time I lived in a small condo in Chicago, and we didn't have a grill so I ended up slow roasting the ribs in the oven. Much to my surprise, the ribs came out tender and delicious. I made them for my dad a few years later and wasn't surprised at all when he asked me how I had made my ribs in the oven. Now my whole family cooks ribs this way.

1 rack baby back ribs
1 teaspoon kosher salt
½ teaspoon black pepper
1 teaspoon garlic powder
barbeque sauce

Heat oven to 250°F and prep the ribs. Make sure to remove the thin membrane on the underside of the ribs before seasoning. Rub with salt, pepper, and garlic powder. Very loosely wrapped the ribs in tin foil and bake them in the oven for 2 - 2 ½ hours. During the last 30 minutes uncover the ribs and brush on a couple layers of barbecue sauce, turning the ribs twice to coat both sides.

Pork Carnitas

Carnitas are a Mexican version of pulled pork, slowly braised for hours until the meat falls off the bone. Then it is shredded and cooked again over a high heat to crisp it up. It is terrific served in a taco shell or atop rice and beans. I think it would also do well in a sandwich or piled on a plate of nachos.

1 4-6 pound pork butt or "picnic ham"
1 large onion, sliced
3 cups chicken stock (water or beer may be substituted)
2 teaspoons dry oregano
1 teaspoon cumin
1 teaspoon kosher salt
½ teaspoon freshly ground black pepper
oil

Heat a tablespoon of oil in a heavy bottomed pan. Season pork with salt and pepper and brown the pork for 4-5 minutes per side. Add onion, oregano, cumin, and chicken stock. Bring up to a boil and cover. Place in a 350°F oven for 3-4 hours or until meat is falling off the bone. Remove from oven and let cool for 30 minutes. Using a fork and tongs, discard fat and bones, and then pull meat apart. Serve with rice and beans.

*Traditionally the meat is returned to a hot frying pan, one portion at a time, and fried in a bit of hot oil over medium high heat until golden and crisped on both sides. The meat is then served in tortilla shells with desired toppings.

Rosemary Crusted Pork Roast

This roast pork recipe is such a breeze...simply season and stick it in a hot oven and you're done. We usually buy a large pork loin and portion it into meal-sized chunks and store the extras in the freezer. This method also works really well with a bone-in rack of pork if you can find one.

2-3 pound pork loin
1 tablespoon dried rosemary
2 teaspoons salt
freshly ground black pepper
olive oil

Preheat oven to 400°F. Season pork with rosemary, salt, and pepper. Drizzle with a bit of olive oil and place on a sheet pan. Insert a digital meat thermometer or have a regular meat thermometer handy for later. Roast meat for 40-50 minutes or until internal temperature reads 155°F and then remove from oven and tent with aluminum foil for 10 minutes. If you have a regular meat thermometer start checking the internal temperature around the 35 minute mark, depending on the size of your roast. Transfer to a cutting board and let rest for 10 minutes before slicing.

At the Cabin

At some point every summer my family would pack up the car and head to my grandparents' cabin in Alpena, Michigan. Often times, we would caravan with my grandparents, aunt, and her significant other, Richard. The cabin was located deep in the woods and did not have any plumbing, running water, or electricity at that time. So we would stop at a gas station nearby to fill jugs with cooking water and enough ice to keep our coolers of food cold during the week.

We spent most of our days taking a little motorboat out on Beaver Lake to fish for bass, perch, and sunfish. What I enjoyed most about that time was listening to the quiet lapping of the waves on the side of the boat and the majestic loons calling out to one another. As for the fishing, we always had good luck. Most of the time there were enough of us that somebody was busy baiting hooks while everyone else was reeling in fish and then we'd trade off when that person tired of handling the worms.

Some days we would explore the land around the cabin. We would take long walks through the trees and stop to look for animal tracks or walk along the trunk of a fallen tree. From time to time we would come across a critter, whether it was a chipmunk, skunk, or porcupine, and we would always be delighted. We would ask questions and my dad would tell us everything he knew about that particular animal.

In the evenings we'd go back to the cabin and make dinner inside the little kitchen. We would drink milk from tall colored aluminum cups and eat together at the table. After dinner we would play cards or checkers for hours and hours. My grandmother always had a grand time playing cards and teaching us her favorite games. While she taught us, she would sit and tell us stories from her childhood.

Her favorite story to tell was about the day she went on a date with a boy from school. He told her they were going to a baseball game, and on the way he stopped along a dirt road and got out of the car. He brought out a guitar and started playing her a song. A bit put out that they weren't going to the baseball game, my grandmother found a new pair of shoes and an ax in his trunk and decided to chop them up while he stood there singing and strumming away. She ended the story by saying that his singing wasn't very good, and then she would chuckle until it brought tears to her eyes and she would have to take a deep breath of air.

When we were tired we would get ready for bed and take turns holding the flashlight as we made our way to the outhouse one last time before bed. Oh, the outhouse, how I disliked that place with it's cold toilet seat and damp toilet paper stored in an old coffee can. I would wait as long as possible before heading out there each night. After we had finished, we would wash our hands, brush our teeth on the porch, and spit the bubbly water into the dirt. The adults usually slept in the rooms downstairs and the kids climbed up to the loft where mattresses were laid out on the floor. We would yell goodnight over and over until we tired of the novelty of sleeping in one big open space and then drift off to sleep.

One particular night I happened to wake in the middle of the night. I had heard a noise and got up to see what I might have heard. I quietly crept down the ladder to the main level and noticed that my dad had looked up from his reading and that mom was starting to stir too. We could hear something crawling around outside, I watched as my dad grabbed an oil lamp and I followed after him as he headed for the front door.

I peered around my dad just as he handed the oil lamp to my mother. She grabbed the lamp and held it up just as my dad pushed open the screen door and bumped into something. Mom positioned the lamp a bit better and my mouth dropped open as I began to understand what I was seeing. What I thought was a raccoon banging around turned out to be a 300 pound black bear and my dad was now standing face to face with it. The only thing separating them was a screen door!

Surprised but not scared, my dad growled deeply and yelled "Get out of here" to scare the bear away. I looked over my shoulder and noticed my brothers were awake too. We all anxiously watched for a few minutes and then listened to my parents retell what had just happened to each other. We could barely sleep that night for fear of the bear coming back and from the excitement of standing so close to a wild bear. I was in awe of my dad who had bravely stood nose to nose with a bear and had actually scared the bear away.

In the morning, we opened the door wide and saw why that bear had been drawn to the cabin in the first place. He had smelled the food in the cooler we had sitting on the porch. During the night he had managed to tear the top right off the hinges and pull out all of the food. Lunchmeat, bread, mustard, and hotdogs were strewn all over the ground. After our close call with that bear we were always a little more weary of keeping our food on the porch and definitely a little more cautious when exploring the woods surrounding the cabin.

I treasure those childhood memories I have of our trips to the cabin because it was a time when we were all together and our only job was to enjoy ourselves and relax. I am so glad my parents made an effort to take us there growing up.

Chapter 7 ✶ Vegetables
and Sides

My mother used to keep a very large vegetable garden filled with tons of wonderful produce. I would help her plant it each spring and I learned so many things from watching each of the seeds we had planted grow into large bountiful plants. In the spring we would pick rhubarb and dip the raw stalks into a bowl of sugar to munch on. In late summer my mother used to make cucumber sandwiches, a favorite of mine, and she would make herself a tomato sandwich with ingredients fresh from the garden.

As a mother, I can find so much value in planting a garden and teaching my children how to grow their own food. Planting a garden has led to so many quality conversations about the foods we eat, and it has helped my children become adventurous eaters.

Zucchini Fritters

These fritters make a great appetizer. They are crispy, crunchy, and cheesy all at the same time. They are easy to make since the vegetables are already cooked, and only require a quick fry. I have made them with my children, and we are done in less than 30 minutes and that is counting clean up time. I know frying can be a little intimidating, but this is a good recipe to try if you are new to frying.

Try this recipe with different vegetables. Our favorites are sweet potatoes, broccoli, and cauliflower.

1 tablespoon olive oil
1 large onion, small dice
1 large zucchini, diced
½ cup flour
½ cup Parmesan cheese
1 teaspoon baking powder
½ cup milk
kosher salt
freshly ground black pepper
oil for frying

Heat olive oil in a skillet over medium heat. Add onions and cook until softened and browned. Remove from heat.

In a large bowl, whisk together the flour, baking powder, and Parmesan cheese. Add the zucchini and onions and stir to combine. Add ½ cup milk and stir to form a thick, paste-like batter.

Heat vegetable or peanut oil in a large heavy saucepan over medium heat until it reaches 350°F. The oil should be about 2 inches deep. Using two spoons, scoop up about a tablespoon of batter and use the second spoon to push the batter into the oil. Fry for 2 minutes per side and then remove and place on a wire rack or plate lined with paper towels. Serve with extra Parmesan cheese.

*Marinara makes a nice dipping sauce depending on the vegetables you choose. I like it best with zucchini and cauliflower fritters.

*Sweet potatoes will need to be peeled, diced, and baked in the oven for 15-20 minutes at 400°F before proceeding with this recipe.

Country Vegetable Stuffing

I like to use leftover bread for the base of this stuffing. It is a great way to use random bits of bread you have in the kitchen. Use this vegetable stuffing for roast chicken, turkey, pheasant, partridge, or bake it in a casserole dish and serve it on the side.

7 slices bread, cubed
2 carrots, peeled and sliced
2 stalks celery, sliced
1 small onion, diced
1 Granny Smith apple, diced
1 egg
1 cup chicken broth
1 tablespoon butter
1 tablespoon olive oil
1 teaspoon salt
½ teaspoon pepper
1 teaspoon poultry seasoning
½ teaspoon fresh thyme

Heat oven to 350°F. Spread cubed bread on a sheet pan and bake until lightly brown. Remove from oven and let cool. In a sauté pan heat butter and olive oil. Add onion, celery, carrot, and apple. Season with salt and pepper. Sauté for 8-10 minutes over medium heat or until vegetables are softened and apple breaks down. Add thyme and poultry seasoning. Mix thoroughly and remove from heat.

In a bowl combine bread cubes and vegetable mixture. In another small bowl whisk together the egg and chicken broth and then pour over bread cubes. Mix to combine. Pour into prepared baking dish and bake for 30-40 minutes.

Joy's Sausage Stuffing

My grandmother, Joy, was a wonderful lady. She was quite opinionated and far from dull. She taught me so many things and made sure that I was exposed to dance, theater, and travel; she wanted to make sure I was cultured. She also showed me how to dip candles, make gingerbread men, and stencil. She was quite skilled.

People have said I have some of her qualities which makes me smile. She was a good cook as well as a baker. She made an irresistible pineapple coconut cake (which reminds me I need to find that recipe!). This sausage stuffing was always her addition to our family's Thanksgiving meal.

1 pound bulk pork sausage
1 large Spanish onion, diced
3 stalks celery diced, small
½ stick of butter
1 loaf of bread, dried and cubed*
chicken or turkey stock
kosher salt
freshly ground black pepper
1 teaspoon sage or poultry seasoning

Boil sausage in 2 cups of water, breaking into pieces as it cooks, set aside. Reserve the water with the meat. Melt butter in a medium skillet and sauté the onion and celery with a pinch of salt and pepper. In a large bowl, combine bread cubes, sausage, cooking water, salt, pepper and sage. Add additional stock if necessary until it is the right consistency. Bread should be moist but not overly saturated or mushy. Bake in a 350°F oven for 1 hour, or until nicely golden on top.

*To dry bread, slice into 1 inch cubes and bake on sheet pans for 15-20 minutes at 300°F.

Roasted Vegetables with Rosemary and Couscous

These roast vegetables make a nice side dish to roast pheasant. You can also add roast pheasant or chicken to the mix and make it into a light meal.

1 large red bell pepper
1 zucchini
1 large onion
2 tomatoes
3 carrots
1 ½ cups sliced mushrooms
2 cloves garlic, minced
2 sprigs rosemary, minced
olive oil
kosher salt
freshly ground black pepper

Chop all vegetables into 1 inch pieces. Lay on a large cookie sheet lined with parchment paper. Generously drizzle with olive oil, salt, pepper, and rosemary. Toss to coat and bake at 400°F for about 20-30 minutes or until tender. Cook couscous per package directions. Toss everything together in a large bowl. Drizzle with a bit more olive oil and taste for seasonings.

*Any combination of vegetables will work and using a different combination keeps it from feeling repetitive. I enjoy adding broccoli, cauliflower, green pepper, and sweet potatoes to change it up.

Della's Scalloped Potatoes

My aunt and grandma make these scalloped potatoes to go with baked ham, and I always looked forward to the combination. The potatoes and onions smell so good baking in the oven all day long.

Don't be afraid to scale this recipe down, it can easily be halved if you do not want leftovers all week long. I only used 4 potatoes and a little over half a can of mushroom soup for the version in the picture to the right and it turned out just fine. I simply reduced baking time to about 1 ½ hours.

10 medium russet potatoes
1 large onion, sliced
1 can cream of mushroom soup
1 cup milk
3 tablespoons butter
1 teaspoon kosher salt
½ teaspoon freshly ground black pepper

Preheat oven to 350°F. Prepare a 9x13 pan with butter. Combine cream of mushroom soup, milk, salt, and pepper in a large mixing bowl. Peel and thinly slice potatoes. Toss potatoes, onions, and milk mixture together to coat. Pour potato mixture into baking dish and place in preheated oven. Bake for 3½ hours or until browned and bubbly on top.

Roast Asparagus

My children love asparagus. Last spring my mother brought fresh asparagus that she had just picked from her garden. I made it for dinner that night, and much to her surprise the kids were fighting over it. On her next visit she did a very smart thing and brought asparagus plants for the kids to plant in the garden so they can have their own fresh supply each spring.

This easy preparation is their favorite way to eat asparagus. Make sure to use tender, in-season asparagus for the best results.

1 pound fresh asparagus, trimmed
olive oil
1-2 tablespoons parmesan cheese
kosher salt
freshly ground black pepper

Place the asparagus in a single layer on a sheet pan. Drizzle with olive oil and season with salt and pepper. Dust with Parmesan cheese and broil for 5-7 minutes or until the asparagus is fork tender. Remove from broiler and sprinkle with additional Parmesan cheese.

New Potatoes with Parsley

I love the hit of fresh parsley in this embarrassing easy side dish. It is the easiest preparation I have for potatoes, but interesting at the same time. Whenever I serve them I always get complimented, which usually surprises me. I think the fresh parsley makes them quite memorable.

2-3 pounds potatoes, new or Yukon gold
2 tablespoons olive oil
2 tablespoons butter
1 teaspoon kosher salt
½ teaspoon fresh ground pepper
¼ cup fresh parsley, chopped

Fill a large pot with water. Add potatoes and bring to a boil and cook for 10-15 minutes, or until fork tender. Drain potatoes and return to pot. Add remaining ingredients and toss to coat. Serve immediately.

Rice with Turmeric

My mother-in-law makes this Middle Eastern rice as a side dish for slow roasted or stewed meat dishes. It is really terrific and so much more flavorful than plain white rice.

1 tablespoon clarified butter*
½ cup thin egg noodles
1 ½ cups rice
3 cups chicken stock or 3 cups water with a cube of chicken bouillon mixed in
¼ teaspoon turmeric
½ teaspoon kosher salt
½ cup slivered almonds
fresh parsley

Soak rice in 3 cups of water for 30 minutes. Drain and rinse with fresh water before cooking.

Melt the clarified butter over medium heat and add the egg noodles. Cook until noodles turn golden brown, stirring constantly. Add the rice and stir to coat. Add all remaining ingredients and bring up to a boil. Cover and move to a preheated 350°F oven for 15 minutes. (I've found it works really well no matter the oven temperature. I've done it anywhere from 325°-375°F with good results.) I have also found that letting it rest with the cover on for 10-20 minutes makes a perfectly delicious pot of rice.

Toast almonds in a small pan oven medium heat. Sprinkle on top of rice before serving. Garnish with fresh parsley.

*Clarified butter can be found in the Middle Eastern aisle of your grocery store and it is often labeled as ghee. If you can't find it, you can substitute with 1 tablespoon melted butter and a teaspoon of olive oil.

Fresh Broccoli with Garlic Chips

Garlic chips are a nice addition to fresh broccoli and elevate a plain vegetable into a delicious side dish with only a little more effort. Watch your garlic closely, since it tends to go from golden to burned very quickly.

4 cups fresh broccoli
¼ cup olive oil
3 cloves garlic
pinch of red pepper flakes
kosher salt
freshly ground black pepper

Steam fresh broccoli until desired tenderness. While broccoli is steaming heat olive oil in a small nonstick skillet. Peel and slice garlic into paper-thin slices. When oil is hot, add garlic slices. Oil should bubble, but it should not be so hot as to burn the garlic. Fry garlic until golden brown. Remove garlic to a paper towel- lined plate to cool. Drizzle hot oil over steamed broccoli, season with red pepper, salt, and black pepper. Serve with garlic chips on top.

*Fresh Parmesan and toasted pine nuts are also tasty additions to this dish.

Ralph and Other Creatures

Growing up on a farm we naturally came in contact with a lot of animals, wild as well as farm variety. There are pictures of me as a toddler with bunnies lying on my belly, holding onto baby ducks, and posing near a rescued fawn. I was too little to remember any of those moments, but I do remember always having some type of baby animal to tend to.

At one time or another we had sheep, horses, chickens, turkeys, geese, quail, pheasants, turtles, pigs, a goat, rabbits, ducks, and two cows named Luke and Duke on our farm. I didn't care for Luke or Duke though. They taught me a hard lesson, and that lesson was that I should never stand behind a cow or horse, even if I am trying to "save" my little brother. It took quite awhile for the side of my face to heal from that lesson.

As for wild animals, there was a time when my brother found a fledgling crow that had fallen out of it's nest a bit too early. He worked on taming the crow, and he carried it around the yard on a leather glove-protected hand. He worked with the crow, Blackjack, until it learned to grip his hand. He tried, quite unsuccessfully, to teach him tricks. After a couple of months the crow had grown strong, and my brother decided to release him into the wild.

Another time we rescued an orphaned baby raccoon and bottle fed it. My mom would make warm bottles of milk mixed with molasses for the cub. She would then give me the bottle with the nipple attached, and I would happily feed it while it nuzzled the bottle and made a purring sound. It quickly grew into a pesky and spirited fellow that we named Ralph. Ralph, being a raccoon, climbed all over the garage and got into the dog food repeatedly, making large messes each time. My mother decided that Ralph was big enough to make it on his own, so she had my dad haul him a few miles away and let him out into the forest.

Not more than a few days later she noticed the dog food scattered all over the garage again. Sure enough, we spotted Ralph scavenging in the garage one night. He had found his way home! My father took him out a bit further and dropped him off. Weeks went by and we didn't see Ralph around the house anymore. However, one day my father was sitting in a tree blind deer hunting. He had a few snacks in his pockets and was pretty surprised when a pesky little raccoon climbed up the tree he was sitting in and started begging for food. Dad instantly recognized Ralph and gave him a few treats and then Ralph wandered off.

A year or two later we saw Ralph one last time. He came back to the house with a few little ones in tow. All along we had thought Ralph was a male, but he was actually a female. We gave her and the babies a little dog food before we shooed them away from the house. From then on we always referred to our old pet raccoon as Ralphina - not Ralph.

Botched Cake Mix

One of the very first things I remember making on my own was a cake mix. My brother Nick and I worked together to read the back of the box and follow the directions. We preheated the oven and floured the pan. We stirred and mixed and then dumped the batter into the pan and waited as the cake baked. Once the buzzer went off we carefully removed the cake and were completely shocked to see that our highly anticipated cake had not risen. Undeterred, we grabbed some spoons and ate our flat cake right out of the pan. It was a little gummy, but not as bad as you might think. Later we realized that we had completely forgotten the eggs! We still laugh about it to this day.

Chapter 8 ✳ Dessert

My grandmother and I used to sit in the clubhouse each fall and peel bushels of apples together. She used to show me how she could peel an apple all the way around and never break the peel. She would hold up the long, curvy, snake-like peel and ask me if I thought I could do that too. I would work hard to peel and turn the apple around and around and I'd usually get two-thirds of the way before breaking the peel.

These days I almost always peel my apples all the way around and I hold up my long, curvy, snake-like peel to show my own kids. I know that before long they will be able to peel their apples as well as I can. It is a tradition I am happy to pass on to my own children.

Apple Danish

My mom is practically famous for her apple Danish. Everyone loves it, including my older brother who has been known to eat nearly an entire sheet pan all by himself. Once he gobbled up a piece my mother had stashed in the house for herself and it nearly brought her to tears when she discovered it missing. To make it worse, my guilty brother didn't seem sorry at all.

crust
3 cups flour
½ teaspoon salt
1 cup vegetable shortening
8-9 tablespoons cold water

filling
1 ½ cups Rice Krispies cereal
8 cups McIntosh apples, peeled, cored, and sliced (6-8 apples)
1 teaspoon cinnamon
½ cup sugar
a pinch of salt

topping
1 egg white
1 cup powdered sugar
½ teaspoon vanilla
milk

In a large bowl, combine flour, salt, and vegetable shortening. Use a pastry cutter to combine until pieces are pea-sized. Sprinkle 6 tablespoons of cold water over flour mixture and gently toss with a fork until dough is moistened. Add additional water a little at a time until dough is moist enough to form into a ball.

Divide dough in half. Generously dust counter with flour and roll dough into a rectangle about 1 inch larger than a 9x13 sheet pan. Gently roll dough around rolling pin and transfer to pan. Unroll and do not trim.

Evenly spread Rice Krispies over pastry shell. In a large bowl combine apple slices, sugar, cinnamon, and salt. Stir well and then evenly pour over Rice Krispies.

Roll out the second ball of dough. Cut vent holes in dough before transferring, place on top of apple mixture. Once transferred, trim, leaving ½ inch extra dough. Roll extra dough under and crimp with your fingers or a fork.

Beat the egg white with a hand mixer until stiff peaks form. Spread mixture over pastry. Bake at 375°F for 45 minutes or until golden brown on top. Remove and let cool to room temperature.

Mix powdered sugar, vanilla, and 2 tablespoons milk together. Drizzle over cooled Danish.

*McIntosh apples cook down into a thick applesauce-like filling that really makes this Danish what it is. Other apples can be substituted, but will change the texture.

*Chex or Corn Flakes can be used in place of Rice Krispies.

Mixed Berry Crisp

I am really drawn to fruit desserts and will choose them over chocolate cake every single time. They are quick to make and a great way to use frozen fruit or any fresh fruit that needs to be used up. Serve with ice cream for an even more delicious dessert.

5 cups mixed berries (raspberries, blueberries, blackberries, strawberries)
¼ cup sugar
1 tablespoon flour

topping
1 cup rolled oats
1 cup brown sugar
½ cup flour
1 teaspoon cinnamon
1 cup butter
a pinch of salt

Combine fruit, flour, and sugar in a large bowl. Transfer to a 2-quart baking dish. In a medium bowl, cut butter into flour and brown sugar using a fork. Mix in cinnamon, oats, and a pinch of salt. Generously sprinkle over fruit mixture. Bake in a 375°F oven for 35-40 minutes or until fruit is bubbly and topping is golden brown.

*I often mix in a peach or two, rhubarb, sweet cherries, or an apple if I need to use something up.

Layered Pumpkin Bars

These pumpkin bars are always a hit at the ranch. They make a festive addition to any fall table. Be sure to use pure pumpkin and not pumpkin pie filling.

crust
1 box yellow cake mix **minus 1 cup**
1 stick butter, softened
1 egg, beaten

filling
1 (29 ounce) can of pumpkin
½ cup brown sugar
3 eggs
¼ cup granulated sugar
⅔ cup evaporated milk
½ teaspoon cinnamon
¼ teaspoon nutmeg

crunch topping
1 cup cake mix
½ stick butter, softened
½ cup sugar
½ cup chopped nuts (walnuts or pecans)

Prepare the crust by mixing cake mix, softened butter, and egg with a mixer until combined. Press into a lightly greased and floured rimmed cookie sheet. Mix the filling ingredients together with a hand mixer or stand mixer. Pour over crust.

To make topping, combine the remaining cake mix, butter, and sugar. Use a fork to cut the butter into the mixture. Stir in chopped nuts. Sprinkle over filling and bake for 50-55 minutes at 350°F or until set.

*Top with whipped cream and additional chopped walnuts. Leftovers should be stored in the refrigerator.

Jean's No-Bake Cheesecake

My Aunt Jean used to make this No-Bake Cheesecake every Christmas, and I always looked forward to it. Some years she would make more than one and let us choose between a blueberry version and a cherry version. I'm not going to lie, I took both, every time.

This cheesecake is very light and airy and no matter what fruit you choose to top it with, just know that you can't go wrong. The cooked raspberry sauce on page 200 also makes a divine topping if you have fresh raspberries on hand.

1 cup crushed graham crackers
6 tablespoons melted butter
½ cup sugar
2 pouches Dream Whip
1 cup milk
2 (8 ounce) packages cream cheese, softened
1 cup powdered sugar

Mix graham crackers and sugar in a medium bowl. Add melted butter and mix with a fork until combined. Press into the bottom of a 9x13 pan. Bake at 350°F for 9-10 minutes. Cool completely.

In a mixer, using paddle attachment, whip cream cheese until smooth. Add powdered sugar. In a separate bowl whip Dream Whip and milk until stiff. Fold Dream Whip mixture into cream cheese mixture. Spread evenly onto cooled crust. Top with raspberry sauce or cherry pie filling.

*You can substitute Cool Whip for the Dream Whip mixture if necessary.

*Feel free to use a different type of pan, such as the fluted tart pan pictured to the right.

Barb's Pecan Pie

My mother makes a delicious pecan pie. She makes this version every Thanksgiving and Christmas, and it is always one of the first things to disappear. My husband loves this pie and looks forward to it every year.

crust
1 ½ cups flour
¼ teaspoon salt
½ cup vegetable shortening
4-5 tablespoons cold water

filling
3 eggs
⅔ cup sugar
½ teaspoon salt
⅓ cup butter, melted
1 cup dark corn syrup
1 cup whole pecans

Preheat oven to 375°F. In a large bowl, combine flour, salt, and vegetable shortening with a pastry cutter until pieces are pea-sized. Sprinkle 3 tablespoons of cold water over flour mixture and gently toss with a fork until dough is moistened. Add additional water a little at a time until dough is moist enough to form into a ball. Generously dust counter with flour and roll dough out into a circle about 1 inch larger than the pan. Gently roll dough around rolling pin and transfer to pie pan. Unroll and trim edges. Crimp with fingers or a fork.

Beat eggs, sugar, salt, butter, and corn syrup in a stand mixer until thoroughly combined. Remove and fold in the pecans. Pour into prepared crust and bake for 40-50 minutes or until filling is set.

*Feel free to substitute chopped pecans or double the amount of nuts if you like your pie filled to the brim with pecans.

AnnaLee's Raspberry Sauce

My aunt has her own raspberry patch and even though she is quite generous with her berries she gets overwhelmed by the shear quantity on a good year. I love it when she does because sometimes she turns the excess into this velvety raspberry sauce that I can (and have) eaten by the spoonful. I think it makes almost anything better.

1 pint fresh raspberries
1 cup sugar

Stir raspberries and sugar in a bowl and let stand for 2 hours at room temperature. Place a sieve over a large bowl and pour raspberry mixture into sieve. Using a spatula, stir and mash berry mixture until all of the juice has gone through the sieve and only the seeds remain. Discard seeds. Raspberry sauce will keep in the refrigerator for up to a week or indefinitely in the freezer.

for a thicker cooked sauce

1 cup sugar
3 tablespoons cornstarch
pinch of salt
3 pints raspberries

Combine sugar, cornstarch, salt, and 2 pints of raspberries in a medium saucepan. Bring to a boil, stirring constantly until thickened. Remove from heat and push through a mesh strainer to remove seeds. Return strained sauce to pan and stir in remaining pint of fresh raspberries. Let cool. Store in the refrigerator for up to a week.

German Apple Cake with Caramel Sauce

My son, Gabe, went nuts for this cake the first time I made it. A few weeks later he asked me to make it again, and he ate so much that he felt sick the rest of the day. I was afraid that would ruin his taste for this cake, much like the time I got sick on egg rolls. However, he still laughs about that day, and he still inhales this apple cake with abandon. He prefers it for breakfast, but I like to serve it for dessert with a good drizzle of caramel sauce and a bit of whipped cream.

2 eggs
½ cup vegetable oil
1 ½ cups sugar
1 teaspoon vanilla extract
2 cups all-purpose flour
2 teaspoons ground cinnamon
½ teaspoon salt
1 teaspoon baking soda
4 cups apples, peeled, cored, and thinly sliced

Preheat oven to 350° F. Butter a 9x13 pan and then dust with sugar. In a mixing bowl, beat oil and eggs with a mixer until creamy. Add the sugar and vanilla and beat well. Combine the flour, salt, baking soda, and ground cinnamon in a bowl. Slowly add this mixture to the egg mixture and beat until combined. The batter will be very thick. Using a wooden spoon, fold in the apples. Spread batter into prepared pan. Sprinkle with 2 tablespoons additional sugar. Bake for 45 minutes or until toothpick inserted in the middle comes out clean. Once cake is cool serve with a dusting of confectioners' sugar and caramel sauce.

Caramel Sauce

½ cup butter
½ cup brown sugar
¼ cup cream
½ teaspoon vanilla

In a medium-sized saucepan, melt butter and brown sugar. Add cream and bring to a boil. Continue boiling for 3 minutes. Remove from heat and add ½ teaspoon vanilla. Let cool slightly before serving with warm cake.

Peanut Brittle

Peanut Brittle is about as fun as it gets when making candy. The ingredient list couldn't be more straightforward, but cooking it is like conducting a science experiment. The sugar syrup erupts like a volcano when the baking soda is introduced and it is quite impressive, albeit a bit scary at the same time. Kids also enjoy the last step of cracking the huge sheet of candy into bits and pieces.

2 cups sugar
½ cup water
1 cup light corn syrup
2 cups raw peanuts
1 ½ tablespoons butter
2 teaspoons baking soda
1 teaspoon vanilla

Bring sugar, water, and corn syrup to a boil in a large pot. Place a candy thermometer in the sugar, be sure it is not touching the bottom of the pan. When the mixture reaches 230°F, also known as soft ball stage, add the peanuts. Continue boiling until the mixture reaches 310°F, at which point it is called hard crack.

Remove mixture from heat and add the butter, baking soda, and vanilla all at once. Be careful as the mixture will erupt and boil rapidly for a few seconds. Mix well and spread on a buttered pan to cool. Once the mixture has cooled completely break it into pieces.

*Be sure to monitor the temperature carefully and do not let it exceed 310°F or it will quickly burn.

Molasses Cookies

Molasses cookies happen to be my favorite cookie. I make them and eat them year round, and I am pretty sure that I have converted my kids as well. If asked, they will still claim that chocolate chip cookies are their favorite, but what self respecting kid wouldn't say that? You won't hear me ask them, though, because I wouldn't want them to feel the need to prove me wrong, as they usually do.

4 cups flour
¾ teaspoon salt
2 ¼ teaspoons baking soda
2 teaspoons ground ginger
2 teaspoons ground cloves
2 teaspoons cinnamon
1 teaspoon espresso powder (optional)
½ cup butter, softened
½ cup vegetable shortening
1 cup sugar
½ cup light brown sugar
½ cup plus 1 tablespoon unsulfured molasses
2 eggs

Preheat oven to 325°F and line two sheet pans with parchment paper. In a large bowl, whisk together the flour, salt, baking soda, ginger, cloves, espresso powder, and cinnamon; set aside. In the bowl of a stand mixer, beat together the butter, shortening, and both sugars until light and fluffy. Beat in the molasses and then add the eggs, one at a time, beating well. Scrape down the bowl after each addition. Slowly add in the flour mixture until combined and no flour remains.

In a small bowl add ½ cup sugar. Roll dough into 1 inch balls (I use a small ice cream scoop) and roll in the sugar.

Place on trays leaving 2 inches between cookies. Bake for 12 ½ minutes. Let cookies cool on the tray for 5 minutes before transferring to a rack to cool.

Date Nut Cookies

I know I said Molasses Cookies are my favorite cookie one mere page prior to this, but I have to say date nut cookies are my favorite holiday cookie. I think part of this is due to nostalgia. To this day, date nut cookies arrive via my aunt and grandmother at every Thanksgiving and Christmas get together. They bring large tins of these dark chewy cookies and everyone inhales them along with the filled cookies on the following page.

They are a tradition and they are part of what makes our holidays complete. I will say that there is no way you or I will ever be able to make these cookies quite the same as my Aunt AnnaLee and my Grandma Degel. They happen to be the only ones that can make these cookies just right. Don't let me scare you though, give them a try, I'm sure they will be quite delicious.

date mixture
2 cups chopped dates
½ cup sugar
½ cup water

1 cup butter
1 cup sugar
1 cup brown sugar
3 eggs
1 teaspoon vanilla
4 cups flour, sifted
1 teaspoon baking soda
1 teaspoon salt
1 teaspoon cinnamon
1 ½ cups chopped walnuts

Combine dates, ½ cup sugar, and water in a saucepan. Cook, stirring occasionally, until mixture is the consistency of very thick jam. Cool completely.

Cream the butter and then add both sugars gradually. On high speed, mix until light and fluffy. Beat in eggs and vanilla. Sift the dry ingredients together. Add to the creamed mixture and blend thoroughly. Stir in the date mixture and the walnuts.

Drop by rounded tablespoons on a greased baking sheet. Bake in a 375°F oven for 14-16 minutes. These get better with time and keep for two weeks or more if stored properly.

Filled Cookies

Growing up I loved eating these cookies during the holiday months. We would get tins of these from my aunt and grandmother, and I always looked forward to biting into the jam filling. I thought it was magical that they could somehow get jam into the center of the cookies. Later I realized that they were actually stacking two cookies on top of each other with jam in the middle. I still found that pretty impressive! It was just like a great big ravioli, but in cookie form. Now that I have my own kids I let them in on the secret, and they enjoy filling these cookies with me every year. They happen to love eating them too.

2 cups sugar
1 cup sour cream
½ cup shortening or softened butter
1 teaspoon vanilla
1 egg
4 ½ cups flour
1 teaspoon baking soda
1 teaspoon baking powder
1 teaspoon salt
jam (raspberry, strawberry, or apricot)

In the bowl of a stand mixer, cream sugar and butter. Add egg, vanilla, and sour cream to mixture. Whisk dry ingredients together in a large bowl. Slowly add dry mixture to wet. The dough should be very soft but not sticky. (I often stop just before it seems ready just to be sure I don't over-beat the dough.)

Flour the counter, turn out the dough, and lightly knead in a little more flour until the dough is no longer tacky. Wrap the dough in plastic wrap and refrigerate for a few hours or overnight.

Remove from fridge 10 minutes before rolling. Roll out a portion of the dough until it is ⅛ inch thick and cut into circles. (I use a drinking glass.) Place a tablespoon of thick jam in the middle. Dip your finger in a bowl of water and run it around the edge of the cookie and then place a second round of dough on top and lightly seal the edges with dry fingers. Bake on parchment lined cookie sheets at 350°F for 7-8 minutes or just until the edges begin to turn color.

*The dough also makes wonderful sugar cookies. Substitute almond extract for the vanilla extract and roll it ¼ inch thick before cutting into shapes. Bake time should be about the same.

Index

A

B

E

Egg(s)

F

Fish

Flour

Fruit, *see also specific fruits*

G

Garlic

Jean's No-Bake Cheesecake, 196

Rice

Rice with Turmeric, 178
Venison Stew, 56
Venison Stuffed Cabbage, 146

S

Salad

Broccoli Salad, 75
Cowboy Caviar, 78
Crunchy Asian Chopped Salad, 72
Macaroni Salad, 70
Potato Salad, 68
Salad in a Jar, 83
Taco Salad, 77
Wilted Spinach Salad, 80

Salmon

Crusted Salmon with Honey Mustard Glaze, 99
Fish Chowder, 52
Salmon Dip, 100
Salmon Patties with Creamed Pea Sauce, 101
Salmon with a Sweet Soy Sauce Glaze, 96

Sauce

AnnaLee's Raspberry Sauce, 200
Creamed Pea Sauce, 102

Sausage

Sausage Gravy, 38
Joy's Sausage Stuffing, 168

Soup

Clam Chowder, 55
Fish Chowder, 52
Lentil Soup, 63
Minestrone, 50
Pheasant Chowder, 58
Venison Chili, 60
Venison Stew, 56

Sour Cream

Filled Cookies, 211
Mushroom Gravy, 140

Spinach

Sweet Corn, Spinach, and Poached Egg with Hollandaise, 29
Fish Packets with Spinach and Leeks, 93
Wilted Spinach Salad, 80

Sweet Potato(es)

Zucchini Fritters, 164
Vegetable Hash Topped with a Poached Egg, 42

T

Tomato(es)
>Lentil Soup, 63
>Minestrone, 50
>Roasted Vegetables with Rosemary and Couscous, 171
>Salad in a Jar, 83
>Taco Salad, 77
>Venison Chili, 60
>Venison Stew, 56

V

Vanilla
>Banana Bread Muffins, 25
>Barb's Granola, 19
>Buttermilk Pancakes, 39
>Crepes, 31
>Date Nut Cookies, 208
>German Apple Cake with Caramel Sauce, 202
>Filled Cookies, 211
>Peanut Brittle, 205

Z

Zucchini
>Minestrone, 50
>Pheasant and Vegetable Pasta, 127
>Pheasant Stir Fry, 114
>Roasted Vegetables with Rosemary and Couscous, 171
>Zucchini Fritters, 164
>Venison Stew, 56

Acknowledgments

I've been dreaming of writing a cookbook for many many years, so when my dad asked me to write one for the ranch I felt like I finally had a reason to start writing. The timing was perfect as my youngest was entering kindergarten, leaving me home alone for the first time in nearly 8 years. Over the past few months I have thrown myself into cooking, writing, and photographing everything you see in this book, and I've been enjoying myself immensely.

So I would like to thank my dad for giving me the push I needed. He has been so encouraging and so excited through the whole process and that has helped propel me through some long days. I would also like to thank my mom for calling to check in on me, answering questions day after day, and for giving me the skills and work ethic to be able to do something this big.

I'd like to thank my brothers for making me tough; without them not a single story in this book would exist. Thanks for jogging my memory and having a good laugh with me while we wracked our brains for every detail from our childhood. Also thanks for always being there, whether it was texting me old pictures or picking apples for me to make into Danish. I know I can ask you guys for anything and you'll be there for me.

I'd also like to thank my husband and sweet children. Gabe, you have such a keen sense of smell and taste that I look forward to your nightly critiques, and I can tell that we will enjoy eating and discussing food for many years to come. Grace, I love how you yell out whatever you think I am making for dinner, especially how you always start by saying "Mom, I know what you're making!" Joseph, my husband, thank you so much for grocery shopping anytime I needed something in the middle of a cooking stint, and for never complaining about eating cold food that has been photographed 47 times. Thank you all for giving me honest feedback and letting me know exactly what you think I should do differently next time. I will never forget that pot pie should always have a top and bottom crust!

Finally, I'd like to thank all of my friends and family for listening to me talk about this project for months and offering to help. AnnaLee, thank you so much for being my proofreader! It's been an amazing process, and I'm lucky to have had so much love and support from start to finish.

About the Author

Katie Khoury was born and raised on a farm in the Thumb of Michigan. She is a certified elementary school teacher, as well as the writer, stylist, photographer, and cook behind the food blog littlespatula.blogspot.com. She has been featured in local newspapers as well as many online publications. She lives in the Chicago suburbs with her husband and two wonderful children.